James David Curran

EXPLORING
ALGONQUIN
PARK

have fun.

Mum, Christmas 1983

♡

EXPLORING
ALGONQUIN
PARK

JOANNE KATES

Douglas & McIntyre
Vancouver/Toronto

Douglas & McIntyre Ltd., 1615 Venables Street,
Vancouver, British Columbia V5L 2H1

Canadian Cataloguing in Publication Data

Kates, Joanne, 1949–
     Exploring Algonquin Park

Bibliography: p.
ISBN 0-88894-378-4

1. Algonquin Provincial Park (Ont.) – Description
and travel – Guide-books.   2. Hiking – Ontario –
Algonquin Provincial Park.   3. Canoes and canoeing –
Ontario – Algonquin Provincial Park.   I. Title.
FC3065.A4K37   917.13′147   C83-091128-6
F1059.A4K37

Design: Barbara Hodgson
Printed & bound in Canada by D.W. Friesen & Sons Ltd.

Acknowledgements

I owe thanks to the following people for significant help in the preparation of this book: Leon Muszynski, Ron Tozer, Dan Strickland, Eugene Kates, John Peters, Kristi Magraw, Alexander Rabazo, Jim Elder, Danny Cotnam, Peter Cziffra, David Soncrant and Paul Campbell.

Contents

*For my grandmothers, who taught me how,
and for Leon, who remembers*

Introduction

This book began in 1932, before I was born. My grandmother, Lillian Kates, was a Toronto matron living in a mansion in the fashionable Rosedale area. Grandad was a dentist and an intellectual. Granny devoted her energies to golf and dinner parties; her two children raised themselves. But during the Great Depression people could not afford to pay their dental bills and Grandad's income dropped to almost nothing. Not being the worrying type, he carried on reading books and fixing people's teeth for nothing, while Granny fussed and fumed about money.

There was nothing for Granny to do but start a business, and for no sane reason she chose to open a children's summer camp. Through clever chicanery, which was to become her trademark, she acquired the lease for a bankrupt nature camp on Tepee Lake in Algonquin Park and opened it in the summer of 1932 with sixty young campers and a ragtag staff, most of them as inexperienced as Granny at camping.

It should not have worked.

But Granny has more than a normal human's share of energy and nerve and she made it work. Camp Arowhon prospered. In 1942 she built a hotel, Arowhon Pines, two lakes away from the camp. When my father came home from the war, Granny moved to the hotel (which she continued to run until she was 81) and my father operated the camp.

I grew up at Arowhon. I took my first steps in Algonquin Park, learned to paddle a canoe shortly thereafter, fell asleep every night listening to the loons on the lake and the mice in the walls, and developed a love of the park that I cannot—and would not—shake. Two factors bias any statements I make about the park: one, it is the home of my heart; two, I own a lease to a cottage there. I spend every free moment from spring until fall in Algonquin Park (and some time in winter too). There is no peace I know more complete than the kind I get from paddling and portaging all day, then watching the sun go down beyond the shore of an Algonquin lake.

I am not the only one. Every year three-quarters of a million people visit Algonquin Park. The park is not a wilderness; there have been people here too long for that. But it is the closest we come in southern Ontario, and to be able to drive for only three hours from Toronto and end up in country that feels like wilderness is the deepest pleasure I know.

Algonquin Park is perched on southern Ontario's highest land. Jack pines cling crazily to rocky lakeshores, and northern spruce meets southern maple here. The maples turn crimson and flame in the fall, and in the spring moose wander along Highway 60. There are more than two thousand lakes within the park's boundaries. It is Ontario's oldest provincial park, born in 1893 of a visionary bureaucrat's dream.

When I was a child, Highway 60, its major artery, was a dirt road. I remember that you could paddle a canoe along the park's rivers for a week and see no other human beings. These things have changed. The highway corridor has been developed, and now there are campgrounds, nature education activities, and even an outdoor theatre. The interior of the park, where canoe tripping takes place, has outhouses and grills on every campsite, and garbage and crowds on many routes.

However, if you know its secrets, Algonquin Park can be a place where the tension between wilderness and civilization is beautifully balanced, where the silence of the back country is only one long portage away from the crowds and the noise. This book aims to tell you how to find the delights of Algonquin Park. For people who are looking for back country as pure as it comes in southern Ontario, there are unspoiled canoe routes in the northern section of the park. For car campers and day trippers, the book outlines the many and diverse amenities of the Highway 60 corridor.

Embarking on a canoe trip without camping and canoeing skills is both uncomfortable and unsafe; I do not recommend it in Algonquin Park or anywhere else. This book will not teach people how to canoe trip, but there are sources of information about canoeing on pages 155-156.

Red Pine Camp, 1982

Joanne Kates

Something will have gone out of us as a people if we ever let the remaining wilderness be destroyed ... We simply need that wild country available to us, even if we never do more than drive to its edge and look in ... [as] part of the geography of hope.

Wallace Stegner (Wilderness, America's Living Heritage)

The Land

A lone canoe glides through the water. The paddles dip and rise in harmony, making only the softest sound of wood against wood, paddle against gunwhale. Across the lake a loon calls. His mate surfaces within spitting distance of the canoe; focussing one cherry-red eye on the evening paddlers, she opens her beak to let out a mournful quaver of a song. Then she dives and is gone.

Such fleeting encounters are the essence of Algonquin Park, for it is one of the rare places to observe wild creatures in their own territories rather than in cages or in the pages of books. It is also the only wild place left in southern Ontario. People need such places just as they need to look up and see an expanse of sky and clouds that is not hedged in by concrete and steel. Wilderness refreshes the mind and the body; it both embodies and symbolizes freedom—freedom from time clocks and technology, from worka-day competition and the complexities of city life. Algonquin Park is a twentieth-century cathedral for the soul, a place where people go in order to feel spiritually whole again. Its values contribute little to the gross national product but much to the sanity of anyone who takes the time to discover them.

But Algonquin Park is not pure wilderness. Most of its forests have been logged at least once; over 2000 km of roads crisscross its interior, and along the highway corridor in its southeastern corner, children's camps, lodges, campgrounds and stores abound. Like other provincial and national parks, it has been set aside as a nature preserve, but humans have made their mark, in commerce, in tourism, and in ecological impact.

That mark is significant. One hundred and fifty years ago the eastern half of Algonquin Park was crowded with white pine trees 60 m tall, having trunks so broad that four men clasping hands could not make a ring around one of them. Some of those pines had been alive for five hundred years. In the mid-1800s there were hundreds of thousands of them; today they number in the dozens. The first pines were felled to become masts and timbers for British sailing ships. Later they came down as the land was cleared and tamed by the pioneers of the New World. To settlers the tall straight pines of Algonquin Park were either resources to be tapped or impediments to civilization. Loggers and farmers never considered that these ancient trees should be preserved.

What remains of the Algonquin forest today, the few virgin pines in the park's heart, the second and third growth forests ringing crystal lakes, are Canada's natural heritage. There is land aplenty in most of Canada, but in southern Ontario, which has the greatest population density in the country, only one place even approximates wilderness: Algonquin Park. Its value can be compared to the value of Westminster Abbey. When the English visit the abbey they seek their ancient heritage; Canadians find their heritage not in buildings but in open-air museums like Algonquin Park.

Yet Westminster Abbey is a mere stripling compared to Algonquin. The jack pines that cling tenaciously to rocky shorelines and put down roots among the grey and black and green lichens where there is almost no soil are growing on the oldest rocks in the world. The park is at the southern tip of the Canadian Shield, which was born 500 million years ago and covers almost half of Canada. At the time of their appearance the rocks of the shield were mountains higher than the Rockies. Geologists tell us they formed from lava that bubbled up from deep within the earth, then cooled and hardened into a granite crust.

About a million years ago the first ice age came to the Canadian Shield. One year the winter temperature dropped lower than it had the year before, and in the following summer a little less winter ice melted. Slowly but surely the glaciers grew until the towering mountain peaks were covered with sheets of ice more than a kilometre thick. Four times the glaciers came and

14

four times they melted, the last time dating ten thousand years ago. Each time the ice receded, millions of rocks imprisoned inside it were released, scouring the mountain surfaces; they scraped the mountains and wore them down until only their roots were left. These roots are the rounded hills that line every Algonquin shoreline today. The movement of glaciers and rocks carved out river valleys and left hollows for lakes. They also left a frigid landscape where nothing grew for thousands of years.

Finally the barren land began to warm. The sun shone on the ancient rocks, and lichens and moss began to grow. Over thousands of years, succeeding generations of these early plants grew, died and decayed to create a meagre soil bed. Then the first pine trees appeared, wrapping their roots around glacial rocks and feeding on the decomposing lichens. As the sun warmed the glacial lakes, they too became hospitable to life. First came reptiles, next fish, and then shorebirds. The first bird was the loon. Along with the grebe, the common loon is the oldest known bird. It has not changed since it first swam on those glacial lakes almost ten thousand years ago.

Leon Muszynski

... *And here were forests ancient as the hills,*
Enfolding sunny spots of greenery.

. . . .

And 'mid these dancing rocks at once and ever
It flung up momently the sacred river.

Samuel Taylor Coleridge (Kubla Khan)

16

The First People

The Algonquin waterways along which modern campers paddle and the campsites where they watch the sun sink behind the rocky hills have been the scene of many voyages predating white settlement in North America. Because the Indians left behind so few signs of their sojourns in Algonquin Park, we sometimes forget that it was their home for thousands of years. By 3000 B.C. there were Indians living within the future park boundaries; archaeologists have found tools and bone harpoons there, and such discoveries indicate the presence of Archaic Stage Indians of five thousand years ago on the shores of Lake Traverse, Grand Lake, Brûlé Lake and Radiant Lake. At Radiant Lake the discovery of butchering tools point to that settlement as a winter hunting camp.

At the northwest end of the park's Rock Lake there are thirty-one rock-lined pits, each barely big enough to accommodate one or two people. They are located about 400 m south of the Madawaska River entrance to the lake and are Algonquin Indian vision pits. During puberty rites and as part of other important life passages marked by rituals, Algonquins would fast for several days on the shores of an isolated lake. Their quest was for a vision of blessing from a spiritual guardian, and they would wait in the vision pit for the spirit to appear.

British and French explorers and missionaries left detailed reports of the Algonquin Indians' lives in the Ottawa Valley of the sixteenth and seventeenth centuries. They were a semi-sedentary people who moved their households each season in order to hunt and gather their food in the most fruitful locations. In summer large bands lived south of the future park where they took advantage of the mild climate and arable land to grow staple crops such as corn. As soon as the days of late summer began to shorten, the bands would break up into smaller groups for travel; each group would put all its possessions in a birch-bark canoe and paddle upriver, via the Petawawa, the Bonne-chere or the Madawaska, into the future Algonquin Park.

During these journeys the women repaired the canoes while the men hunted ducks and caught fish for winter storing, and the children picked blueberries for drying. At night they set up portable bark-covered wigwams. They timed their arrival at their winter camping grounds on the shores of a big lake, such as Opeongo, Cedar or Laveille, before the snow fell, and there they would build bark lodges, each having a fire pit in the centre with a smokehole above it. At night they kept warm under rabbitskin robes; by day the men would work their way around the shores of the lake and up its tributary rivers following animal tracks, hunting for moose and rabbit.

By the time the days started to lengthen, the supply of dried blueberries and fish would be exhausted. As the trees began to leaf and the snow melted, animal tracks were no longer easy to follow. The Algonquins prepared to leave their winter hunting camps and head south again—but not before the sap was running from the sugar maple trees. The Indians collected the sap, boiled it in birchbark vessels (later they would use iron pots) and stored the resulting sugar for the next winter. By then the women would have finished making new birchbark canoes. Now the ice was gone from the rivers and it was time to paddle back the way they had come in the autumn.

Not until the seventeenth century did the Algonquin Indians feel the influence of whites, and at first this influence was indi-rect. The Iroquois tribes to the south of Lake Ontario had been trapping beaver and selling the pelts to European fur traders. They had grown accustomed to the goods they received in return for pelts, and when the beaver were trapped out in their tradi-tional territory, the Iroquois moved north where the animals were still plentiful. So it was that the Iroquois invaded the terri-tory of the peaceable Algonquins, forcing them northward. Iroquois stayed in the future park trapping beaver until well into the eighteenth century, when they moved south again to fight with the British against the French in the Seven Years war. The Algonquins then resumed their previous habit of wintering in the park, but it was not to be theirs for long.

The fashion of wearing furs had spread among wealthy Europeans, and by the end of the eighteenth century their traditional sources of fur—the countries bordering on the Baltic Sea—were almost trapped out. Because of the increasing scarcity, the price of Baltic pelts rose and British fur traders began to seek more economical supplies farther afield. In the New World the beaver, the marten and the coveted mink were still in good supply, and it was the search for their pelts that brought the first white men to Algonquin Park. It never became a major fur-trading area, but the traders' tales inspired other Europeans to explore its forests and rivers.

The first white man to paddle through the future park was Lieutenant Catty of Britain's Royal Engineers. In 1818 he was on assignment to find a way to transport soldiers between Ottawa and the upper Great Lakes. The reason for Catty's Algonquin assignment was the uneasiness that Britain felt towards her southern neighbour, having recently fought two wars in the New World: the American Revolution in 1776 and the War of 1812 against the United States. But it was not the transport of troops to defend Upper Canada against the Americans that was to determine the next step in the life of Algonquin Park, for Britain made peace with America. Instead there were other events half a world away that would have a profound influence on this portion of land.

My axe and I – we do immortal tasks –
We build up nations – this my axe and I
Isabella Valancy Crawford (Song of the Axe)

Birth of the Park

In 1800 Britain was entering a great period of mercantilism, spurred by the Industrial Revolution at home. In order to extend its trade around the world, Britain needed large timbers to build a trading fleet. Towards the end of the eighteenth century Britain had two traditional sources of ships' timbers: the American colonies, and the Baltic countries of northern Europe. In 1776 the American Revolution had ended the flow of pine timbers from New England; and in 1808 Napoleon Bonaparte of France, who was at war with Britain, set up a naval blockade, successfully preventing his enemy from trading with the Baltic countries.

Meanwhile, British fur traders and explorers such as Lieutenant Catty had brought home the news that the Ottawa Valley, and particularly the area of the future Algonquin Park, was rich with pine trees. It was an English fur trader with a post on Golden Lake (just outside the present park) who persuaded the Algonquins to allow the first timber cruiser, Alexander Macdonnell, to enter their territory and survey it for logging. Had the Indians guessed how much logging would alter their home territory, it is doubtful they would have been so kind as to draw him a map of the land.

Britain needed those white pines to assure its trading fortune, and it took them; by 1912 almost none was left standing. The Ottawa Valley became the centre of the burgeoning Canadian lumber industry, and Algonquin Park was its heart. Until 1830 the area was wilderness; by 1846 five thousand square kilometres of land in and around the future park were being logged

21

Public Archives of Canada (C-25718)

Camboose shanty

for the big pines. Logging changed the area's natural landscape completely.

An early logger lived the life of a pioneer. When a new camp was needed the men broke trails into raw bush and cut trees to build it. They constructed camboose shanties from one end of the park to the other where they lived in winter while felling trees and preparing them to be floated down the rivers in spring. Camboose shanties were built to one simple design: a large log cabin used as a bedroom, kitchen, dining room and recreation room all in one. The name camboose (from the French "cambuse"—a food storeroom) referred to the central fire that burned under the smokehole in every shanty.

The roaring fire was never out, and a good thing that was, for it drew the musty smells of drying clothes, the cooking smoke and the acrid odour of green tobacco from every corner of the shanty and upwards, functioning as an excellent chimney and ventilator. That fire was the only source of heat and light all winter, so the beds were built in tiers around it. It was also the cooking fire, and in every shanty the cook was boss. No talking was permitted during meals, which were large but monotonous, consisting of fried salt pork —the men called it "Chicago rattlesnake"—beans and molasses. All of the shanty's supplies came by wagon or sleigh from the Ottawa Valley, except for the occasional vegetable crops grown on park depot farms (such as the one at Sunnyside on Opeongo Lake).

Lumberjacks went to shanty in the fall of each year and worked from sunrise to sunset six days a week felling the great pines with their saws and axes. After each tree was felled, the skilled woodsmen would cut off its branches and then square it. The timbers had to be squared so that when they were loaded into the holds of ships bound for Britain they could be piled securely on top of each other to keep the loads from shifting in the vicious North Atlantic storms and reducing the ships' stability. Once the logs were squared they were loaded onto sleds and wagons and "skidded" or dragged by teams of horses out of the woods to the rivers where they would await spring breakup.

As soon as the winter's ice melted, all the large rivers of the park—the Nipissing, the Petawawa, the Madawaska and the Opeongo—became highways for moving the timbers downstream. As the logs entered the wide lower reaches of the rivers they were fastened together into rafts which were floated down the Ottawa River to Quebec City. There the rafts were taken apart and the logs loaded onto outbound sailing ships.

The river drive was a perilous operation, for when warm weather melts the prodigious Algonquin snowfall, the rivers are swollen with fast water. The huge square timbers were whirled along at a fearsome speed, often piling up in huge logjams. It would then be the drivers' job to walk along the logs on the river to break up the jam. A driver who failed to calculate the moment at which an immobile logjam would become a maelstrom of fast-moving logs would be crushed or drowned, and there are crosses at the foot of many Algonquin rapids to record the death of unlucky river drivers.

Being able to use and control the spring flow of river water was crucial to the loggers, who built dams and log chutes on the park's rivers. The function of the chutes was to use water flow to speed logs past an obstruction in a river, such as a shallow rapids, and the dams were used to hold back water in the early spring and then let it flow downstream under control for the most efficient propelling of the logs.

When the Ontario government sent out survey teams to the Algonquin area as a prelude to its agricultural settlement, the lumber companies began to worry. Settlement and agriculture did not mix with logging, for several reasons. Farmers often dam and divert rivers for their own purposes, such as irrigation, which would reduce the loggers' much-needed water flow. And where there are settlers there have always been forest fires, which devour valuable stands of timber. So when the Ontario government began to consider turning a large part of the land west of the Ottawa River into a nature and forest preserve where settlement would be excluded, the logging companies were very supportive.

This idea had been born in the mind of a government surveyor named James Dickson in 1882 when he conducted a survey of the township of Canisbay, now inside the park. He was to survey the area for settlement, but unlike most of his colleagues in government, Dickson thought the area far too rugged for agriculture and felt it would be an ideal recreation area. In 1885 Alexander Kirkwood, another Ontario government employee, wrote to the commissioner of crown lands suggesting a provincial park for the area, and Dickson followed up Kirkwood's letter by beginning to survey the possible park site. In 1892 a Royal Commission was set up to investigate the possibility of creating what Kirkwood had already begun to call Algonquin Park, and in 1893 the Commission submitted its report in favour of the park's creation.

Dickson and Kirkwood's campaign was aided by the logging industry's support. Ontario's first provincial park promised to be good for loggers: settlers would be excluded; the headwaters of rivers would be protected, and the government would be responsible for fighting the forest fires that were causing the companies a good deal of lost revenue. E.H. Bronson, one of the Ottawa Valley's biggest lumber barons and a member of the Ontario cabinet in 1893, praised the notion of a provincial park on behalf of the logging industry.

Algonquin Park was created by order of the Algonquin Park

Act in 1893, which stated that it was to be "a public park and forest reserve, fish and game preserve, health resort and pleasure ground for the benefit, advantage and enjoyment of the people of the Province." The provincial government then ruled that the loggers could continue cutting in the new park until all the pine was removed. The present-day Algonquin Park multiple-use policy has its roots in the historical relationship between the logging companies and the Ontario government, and in the Act of 1893, which set up the new park with an explicit promise to serve both loggers and recreational users.

Even a century ago some people disagreed with such large-scale logging practices. Henry David Thoreau wrote about the logging of big pines that it was "as if individual speculators were to be allowed to export the clouds out of the sky, or the stars out of the firmament, one by one." But Thoreau's voice was in the minority, and the logs were needed to feed the insatiable market of the growing North American cities. Smaller pines were in demand for furniture and for the building of houses, so the loggers began cutting the smaller trees. In order to turn these trees into sawlogs, mills were required; the lumber companies built sawmills throughout the park, from Canoe Lake in the south to Kiosk in the north. With every sawmill came mill workers, their families, schools, churches, hospitals, missions and stores.

In 1913 the Ontario government responded to political pressure from J.R. Booth, who owned timber rights to much of Algonquin Park, and passed an "Act to Confirm Certain Agreements Respecting the Limits of J.R. Booth in Algonquin National Park." By that act Booth and the other loggers were permitted to cut every species of tree. Without restrictions on what they could cut or where, the logging companies and the mills prospered.

That period was the great age of development in the park. The mill villages grew; by 1920 there were two new rail lines running through the park, and three luxurious railway hotels had been built (on Cache, Smoke and Burnt Island lakes). Other lodges as well as children's summer camps were constructed, fishing camps were opened, and leases were issued to cottagers.

In spite of both the logging and the recreational development, much of the park's land was still unspoiled during the 1930s, for

Ron Reid

several reasons: recreational development was restricted to the small area having easy access to the railroad lines, there being few roads and no highway. As for logging, the axe and the river imposed natural limits on the scale of logging operations and on the loggers' methods, which were essentially in harmony with the park's environment. These limits, however, were short-lived.

During the Depression of the 1930s the government hired crews for two make-work programs in Algonquin Park. The first involved drowned shorelines that the loggers had created when they built dams and flooded lakes in order to tailor watercourses to the needs of their spring river drives. The crews cleared away the dead trees from those shorelines.

The program was purely cosmetic, but the government's second project changed the park beyond recognition. In 1933 crews began building a highway through the park, which was completed in 1936. It brought cars into the park and brought logging trucks and bulldozers to replace the river drives. And with the highway came pressures that have since made the balance between people and nature ever more uneasy.

The Uneasy Balance

... this great green girl grown sick
with man   sick with the likes of us ?

. . . .

ankles rashed with stubble
belly papulous with stumps?

Earle Birney (Transcontinental)

The year that Earle Birney wrote that poem about Canada was a year of change for Algonquin Park as technology began to have its effect, and the changes rang loud in the quiet forest. The chainsaw, invented during World War II, was first used there in 1945, and that was also the year of the last spring river drive down the Petawawa River. Trucks began to haul timber along the newly built highway. For the first time the park was open to tourists in cars, and the postwar economic boom brought crowds. The railway line was rendered redundant; fewer and fewer trains ran through the park, until the line closed altogether. The logging companies began to develop a network of roads, and these together with new machinery allowed them to expand their scale of operations. By 1973, 95 percent of Algonquin Park was under licence to be logged by twenty-three logging companies, and over 2000 km of roads had been built.

On the recreational level, too, the park's development was proceeding at a breakneck pace, and little consideration was given to what constituted appropriate use of a provincial park. During the 1950s and '60s people were permitted to fly into fishing camps, and there were no controls on the use of powerboats or on waterskiing at any of the lakes.

Lunch on Opeongo Lake, 1930s

Ontario Ministry of Natural Resources (AFM 95)

In September 1965 Douglas Pimlott, a University of Toronto zoologist, called a meeting of other concerned people to express his dismay at how the park's forests were being affected by logging methods. Out of that meeting grew the Algonquin Wildlands League, committed to fight for the survival of this threatened wilderness area. The league members wanted logging ended in Algonquin Park, which they believed should be restored to its wild state. Working with the Federation of Ontario Naturalists and other citizens' organizations, the league conducted a far-reaching campaign of public education on parks and wilderness. The lumber companies countered with their own campaign; they accused the conservationists of being "canoeing elitists" from Toronto who knew nothing about the real interests of the Algonquin area. The controversy became a political battle between the conservationists and a coalition of powerful forces: the logging companies, who have traditionally maintained close ties with the provincial government, and members of parliament from the logging towns that surround the park.

28

The task of determining the future of the park fell ironically to the provincial Ministry of Natural Resources, whose main mandate is to extract and market natural resources, principally minerals and forest products, from Ontario's land.

The contradiction between extracting resources on the one hand and protecting them on the other hand is a difficult one to resolve. In 1974 the ministry introduced the Algonquin Park Master Plan, a blueprint for the management of the park until the year 2000. The plan stated that the park would provide recreational opportunities and a protected environment with the constraint of also providing "sufficient forest products to sustain dependent industries at current levels of utilization." The conservationists had lost their battle.

The Master Plan created a zone system for the park in order to protect both natural and historical areas. However, the main primitive zone where logging is not permitted comprises only 8.9 percent of the park's total area and is adjacent to the Highway 60 development zone. The natural zones comprise only 4.3 percent of the area, and the historical zones, only 0.4 percent; 74.9 percent of the park's land may be logged.

Although the plan calls for the phasing out of the park's 350 cottage leases, this will not alter the park's ecology a great deal since the majority of cottages are concentrated in the Highway 60 development corridor, which will not in any case be returned to wilderness.

On the positive side, the Master Plan called for the banning of cans and bottles in the park's interior, and it also set limits on the number of groups permitted to enter the interior from each access point. The plan restricted waterskiing to eleven cottage lakes and permitted motorboat use on only twenty-seven of the park's lakes. And instead of leaving control over logging in the hands of private companies, it put all logging under a crown corporation, the Algonquin Forestry Authority.

Although conservation groups were dismayed by this blueprint, which still permitted logging, and the Provincial Parks Council, an Ontario government agency, demanded a number of changes—that the park's wilderness and primitive areas be increased to 31 percent, that recreation take precedence over logging, and that the public be given input into park logging policy in 1979 the five-year review left the zones exactly as they were in 1974 and did not reduce logging in the park. And there had been no real opportunity for public input.

The current Forest Management Plan was unveiled in the spring of 1981 and is impressive in its outline for efficient and careful harvesting of the Algonquin forest, using the most modern silvicultural methods, which are designed both to regenerate the forest as it is logged and to make the minimal impact on the park. One of the most significant aspects of the plan is the way in which it separates logging from the recreational users of the park, both in time and in space. Logging is not permitted within 30 m of any shorelines or within 60 m of portages and hiking trails. There are also legally required sound buffer zones; on July and August weekends, for example, loggers are not permitted to use noisy machines to construct roads or to haul wood by truck within 1.6 km of canoe routes. All the park sawmills have been closed. There are strict limitations on where the Forestry Authority is permitted to build new roads. This limitation often results in temporary roads being built over a stream immediately after the canoe tripping season ends in fall and being used all winter; then the crossing is removed and the banks replanted in time for the next spring's canoe season. Because of the great care taken to shield recreational users from logging operations, park visitors now encounter few signs of logging.

Logging in Algonquin Park is far less obvious than it was before the Forest Management Plan was put into effect, but it is no less pervasive. The care taken to shield recreational users from the sight of logging has a Disneyland effect, like the façade of a wild West town that is erected as a movie set but has no buildings behind it. The incompatibility between a provincial park and logging has been camouflaged but not eradicated, and the crucial question is whether a provincial park should be a tree farm, even a well-managed one.

There have also been serious questions raised about the increased dependency of local logging companies on Algonquin timber. Recently the Authority has begun to permit the cutting and marketing of wood for pulp, and by the year 2000 twice as much timber will be cut, reflecting the involvement of yet another dependent industry, this one created by the Authority

Joanne Kates

itself. This practice is questionable because the Master Plan stipulated that Algonquin Park had to supply lumber to "dependent industries," but it did not give authority to create more of them.

Another problem is that silvicultural practices of regeneration and selective cutting have not existed long enough for foresters to know how they affect forest growth in the long term. There is always the possibility that altering a forest artificially will cause the extinction of entire species of plants and animals that depend on specific habitats for their survival. Nor is there a way of knowing what happens to a forest when its soil is deprived of the complex organic diversity that it derives from dead trees as they fall and rot. We do know the effect of the Forestry Authority's approximately 2000 km of roads in the park: trucks travelling along them at speeds of up to 100 km/h frighten wild animals and drive them away from their natural paths.

Although logging in Algonquin Park creates jobs for a large number of people, there may be enough marketable timber within a 100-km radius of the park to replace the timber being cut there. But because of the Algonquin Forestry ·Authority's efficient management, government has not had to look elsewhere for new sources of wood. Conservationists point to similarities between Algonquin and Quetico parks; in the case of Quetico, when logging was stopped there the logging companies found the trees they needed outside its boundaries. It is quite possible that the same could be true of Algonquin.

There is a limit to how long any one piece of land can be logged. "Sustained yield" harvesting is not perpetual harvesting; maple and birch trees do not regenerate even in a human generation but take centuries to reach full growth.

Logging has taken place in Algonquin Park for more than a century. Species by species its trees have been removed: first the large pines, then the spruce and hemlock and yellow birch, and now the maple trees. Time may be running out for the trees, and if it is, it is also running out for the birds and the animals—and for us.

Today's Concerns

At twilight in the park I always know I am home when the lake echoes with the maniacal quaver of the local loons. So it is with great pain that I write of the danger to loons, and indeed to all of the life forms in Algonquin Park. Quite simply, acid rain is killing the park.

Acid rain is produced by the burning of fossil fuels. When coal, oil or gas are burned they produce acids that travel on the winds for thousands of kilometres. The greatest producers of airborne acids are industrial users of fossil fuels, and Algonquin Park gets acid rain borne on storms from as far away as Chicago and Pittsburgh, as well as from the tall stacks that vent nickel mills in nearby Sudbury.

The park is more vulnerable to acid rain than are most other parts of southern Ontario because the rocks of the Canadian Shield do not contain materials, such as limestone, that buffer or absorb the acids. When a lake becomes acidic, aluminum, mercury and other poisonous metals which have been stored in the soil are released and then consumed by the small organisms at the bottom of the lake's food chain. Fish that feed on those small organisms store the poisons in their bodies. Mature fish do not necessarily die from the poisons but their ability to reproduce begins to weaken. Two species of fish most sensitive to the effects of acid rain are trout and bass—the two predominant fish species of Algonquin Park. At first the fish fail to spawn; then they begin to die off. As fish populations decline, animals that depend on fish for their survival begin to decline too.

Ontario Ministry of Natural Resources

The Loon, the Loon,
Hatched from the Moon

Writhes out of the lake
Like an airborne snake.

He swallows a trout
And then shakes out

A ghastly cry
As if the sky
Were trying to die.

Ted Hughes (Under the North Star)

Loons are particularly vulnerable to the effects of environmental pollution because they are predators at the top of a food chain: their diet consists of large fish which in turn have eaten small fish which have eaten insects which have eaten algae. Every time a loon eats a fish it receives the entire load of environmental poison that the fish has consumed and stored during its lifetime. For the loons acid rain is double jeopardy: as the number of fish declines they have trouble getting enough to eat; and the fish they eat are contaminated. The poisons in their diet cause birds to lay thin-shelled eggs and these break instead of hatching.

Even if the loons were to eat a safe diet in Algonquin Park, they would still be in danger from environmental pollution because they spend their winters south of the park on the Atlantic coast where they live on fish whose flesh is loaded with pesticides.

Park naturalists estimate that if acid rain continues to fall, there will be neither loons nor fish in the park by the year 2000. All the animals that nest in the water or feed on fish will be gone, including frogs, otters, ducks, herons and beavers. In fact, this prediction has already begun to be fulfilled. Because of the effects of acid rain, not one trout was born in Algonquin Park in 1976. The culprit that year was the acidity of the meltwater which flows into the lakes in spring. On hot spring days so much acid snow melts that the top layer of every lake in the park is acid. When the trout rise to the surface to feed and to fill their air bladders with oxygen, they are poisoned and cannot spawn. The danger is compounded when springtime temperatures soar. On Easter weekend in 1976 the temperature in Algonquin Park reached 26°C and the shock of acid meltwater hitting the lakes was devastating. Not only did the trout fail to breed, but frogs and salamanders and other animals that breed in pools of water created by spring runoff were also poisoned and could not reproduce.

If we do not act swiftly to reduce the worldwide emission of industrial airborne acids, we will have to tell our grandchildren stories about the beaver and the otter, the frog and the salamander; and we will have to play them recordings of the loon's call, for they will never hear that sound.

Individual concern alone cannot eliminate the threat posed by acid rain to the forests and lakes, but Algonquin Park is equally endangered by other forms of pollution which individuals *can* do something about. The balance between people and nature is often uneasy in a park, and when that balance goes awry, the very purpose of the park is threatened.

Parks like Algonquin are created to protect nature and to offer people the pleasure of seeing wild animals and plants in their natural environments. When people leave behind evidence of their presence, the park is no longer natural. On every portage and campsite in Algonquin Park you will see garbage, from plastic bags and tin cans to toilet paper and feces. If this beautiful wild place is not to become an exurban garbage dump, users must learn the meaning of Zero Impact Camping—to leave nothing behind but footprints.

Consider what would happen if every one of the park's annual three-quarters of a million users discarded two or three small pieces of trash: the forests would soon be unusable for recreation. It is important to carry out every single piece of nonburnable garbage.

And just as garbage is piling up on the land, it is also threatening the lakes. Because water pollution is invisible, it is easier to ignore; but such pollution is more dangerous, for it affects the health of people who swim in the water and drink it. At heavy-use parks in the United States, backpackers are beginning to report cases of dysentery from bacteria-infected water, the result of poor toilet habits on the part of campers. Algonquin Park has only a thin layer of soil covering its glacial rock and anything left within 50 m of a lakeshore runs downhill into the water the first time it rains.

Most Algonquin campsites have outhouses; if one is available it should always be used. In the absence of an outhouse, walk at least 50 m from the water, dig a hole 15 cm deep (the soil is soft enough to do this with the heel of a shoe), and then bury your feces and toilet paper. Otherwise you could be responsible for releasing dysentery-carrying bacteria into the lake.

The camper who wishes to preserve this wilderness park for future generations will take the trouble to carry biodegradable soap and use it for all washing. This soap is easily obtainable at health food and outdoor stores. Be sure to dump all soapy water, even from biodegradable soap, at least 50 m from any lake.

Zero Impact Camping, the digging of privies where necessary, and the use of biodegradable soap may seem to be troublesome distractions to the wilderness experience, but in fact they are insurance against the disappearance of the wilderness. The impact that human beings make on the park is enormous; and with the number of canoe trippers and hikers rising every year the park's landscape is changing for the worse. People are beginning to threaten the very existence of the natural environment they seek. They must stop cutting down live trees, damaging the forest by camping outside of designated campsites, and polluting the interior peacefulness with noise. As Edward Abbey wrote in 1973: "Our children may someday read of the American wilderness . . . as we read of lost Atlantis." Time is not on our side. And Algonquin Park is too precious to squander.

Painted Trillium

. . . of golden sands, and crystal brooks,
With silken lines, and silver hooks.
There will the river whispering run
Warmed by thy eyes, more than the Sun.

John Donne (The Bait)

Spring

At the end of April there are still pockets of snow in the hollows of Algonquin Park, but the sun is now strong enough to coax the trout-lilies into bloom. These large, nodding yellow flowers are among the first to appear in the maple forests. By June their blossoms will have vanished as the trees leaf out, creating a canopy of shade and denying the lilies the source of light they need in which to bloom. May is the best time to see wildflowers in the park. Spring beauties—tiny, white five-petalled flowers, each petal striped with fuschia —carpet the forest floor. Often as early as Easter trailing arbutus can be found in pine woods. Short, stocky plants with thick oval leaves, they have small white or pink blossoms that emit a spicy fragrance. In the park's wet-lands, along shorelines and in bogs, you will find the metre-high evergreen shrub called leather-leaf. During much of the year only its green, oval leathery leaves can be seen, but in May this plant produces miniature white bell-like flowers. A bit later two varieties of trillium appear: one red and one painted (white with crimson streaks). Late spring is also the time to look for the delicate plant with pink bell-shaped flowers on a crooked stem, aptly called twisted stalk.

From the end of May until the end of June the hardwood trees get their leaves and thus fewer wildflowers are to be found beneath them. But Algonquin is a rare transition zone between northern and southern vegetation and includes not only the hardwoods typical of more southerly regions but also coniferous forests of the north, and each forest type encourages a different sort of wildflower. The conifers—pine, spruce, hemlock, fir, cedar, tamarack—never give as much shade as the hardwoods; their soil tends to be sandier and more acidic, and this, too, influences the flower population.

In late spring fifteen different species of violet bloom in the park's coniferous forests, their flowers ranging in colour from white, yellow and blue to deep violet. Now the unassuming bunchberry begins to blossom. Low to the ground, with a cluster of oval leaves radiating from a central axis which produces a small, four-petalled white bloom, bunchberry flowers gain splendour by their large numbers. Canada mayflowers are often found in the same terrain. Their tiny, white bell-shaped flowers are of no particular distinction, but their fragrance is so strong that it permeates the evergreen woods in June, hence its other common name, wild lily-of-the-valley. Twinflowers also inhabit these forest floors; their pink, bell-shaped flowers are sweet-scented and always found in pairs. The fringed polygala (also known as gaywings) is far less common, but its exotic petals are worth looking for in damp coniferous woods, especially on Algonquin portage trails during late May and June. Its bright magenta flower has a long central cylindrical section with two "wings" growing from its base and fringes at the ends. By the time gaywings and twinflowers are blooming, new growth is beginning to show on the pines, firs and cedars, their growing tips a bright, fluorescent green.

But spring in Algonquin Park is more than vivid, sparkling colours; it is also a time of sounds, both musical and functional. Everywhere, on land, in the water and in the air, birds and frogs sing their mating songs and musically proclaim their territories. On a sunny spring day hundreds of birds make themselves heard: kinglets, ducks, swallows, flickers, sapsuckers, woodcocks and more. From the undergrowth comes the startling sound of a distant motor going into action—actually the rapid wing-beat of a ruffed grouse as he "drums" to attract a mate. Perhaps the sound most synonymous with spring is the bright, repetitive song of the white-throated sparrow, which consists, according to Roger Tory Peterson (*Field Guide to the Birds*), of "several clear, pensive whistles, . . . one or two clear notes, followed by three quavering notes on a different pitch." The male white-throated sparrow considers nearly a hectare of forest to be his territory, and he brooks no intrusions there; his song warns other males to leave or be attacked. Researchers, playing tape recordings of other bird songs to the white-throat have discovered that he recognizes the sound of his neighbours' songs. If a neighbour bird strays into a white-throat's territory he neither threatens nor attacks; but if a recording of an unknown white-throat's song is played in the same spot, the bird whose territory it is sings angrily and may even attack the tape recorder.

If the white-throat's song is the music of an Algonquin spring day, then the frogs' courting chorale is pure nightmusic. After dusk, when the melancholic chant of the whip-poor-will is heard, the frogs begin their chant, which continues until dawn. The male frogs sing to attract female frogs and to warn other males to respect their territorial boundaries. Frogs are fiercely territorial, willing to fight for and protect the best mating spots. An eastern gray tree frog's territory may be only half a square metre of midnight swamp, but a male trespasser risks attack.

Particularly after a rainstorm the frogs are in fine voice, and with a little practice it is possible to identify the songs of the five most common frogs and toads among the hundreds of voices. Easily identifiable are the spring peepers (they peep monotonously hour after hour); the green frog plunks like a banjo, the treefrog trills, the American toad sounds like an operatic soprano, and the bullfrog croaks at the bottom of the register. Nothing can quite match a symphony of frog songs on a starry night in June.

But the frog symphony is short-lived; as soon as the mating season has been completed, the nights are silent again. For the same short period—from the end of May until the final days of June—some of the park's birds sport dazzling mating plumage. Large flocks of evening grosbeaks brighten the forests with their yellow bodies and black and white wings. Beside every springtime stream and marsh redwing blackbirds perch on cattails, flaunting their scarlet epaulets. Their cacophonous song and the display of their epaulets warn other males to respect their territories.

While the redwings are courting, the herons arrive from the south to mate and nest in the park. The great blue heron is a magnificent bird with a wingspan of almost two metres and a

Ontario Ministry of Industry & Tourism

Redwing blackbird

long neck. Most of the year it is a loner, disdaining the company of its kind. Male and female blue herons cannot even tell each other apart on sight and require an elaborate set of behavioural signals in order to communicate with each other. Only during the spring nesting season do blue herons congregate and then solely for mutual protection against predators. They nest together in noisy treetop colonies called heronries, which are often built in white pine trees on islands and may include as many as twenty-five nests. In the park there is a heronry on Johnston Lake, near the Barron Chute, and one on Erables Lake in the north.

But perhaps the bird most frequently associated with Algonquin Park is the loon. Loons return to the park each spring soon after breakup and begin their courting ritual. Two loons—males and females look almost exactly alike—will either race wildly across the water or swim slowly towards each other, then point their bills to the sky. Loons mate monogamously for life and tend to return to the same lake for nesting every year, often to the same nesting site.

These birds move with the greatest difficulty on land: to facilitate swimming, evolution has positioned their legs so far back on their bodies that they literally cannot walk but use their legs to push themselves as they skid along on their bellies. Thus loons must build their nests just barely above the water line and are vulnerable to changes in water levels. The park has twenty-seven dams whose water flow is regulated for various reasons; five of them are controlled to give water power to Ontario Hydro plants downstream. Although care is taken to avoid damaging nesting sites, it is inevitable that sometimes loons' nests are flooded.

Nesting begins in early June. Each loon lays two eggs and both parents take turns incubating them. In early July the chicks hatch and shortly thereafter take to the water, although the first few times out they may ride on their mother's back. Both parents spend the summer teaching the chicks how to fish. A loon can easily dive 25 m below the water's surface; it can swim faster than most fish and can pivot underwater with the speed and grace of a trout. The loon is completely at home in water; it both catches and eats its fish underwater and sleeps on its surface, protected by its waterproof plumage.

Flying, though, is the loon's bête noir, for in the process of evolution, its wings were designed to be folded away for swimming, not used for flying. A loon's maximum airspeed is 100 km/h; it flies low and cannot take off from land, as most birds can. With approximately ten fish in its belly, this bird needs at least half a kilometre of lake runway to take off. It is a common sight to see a loon running along a lake surface, beating the water with its wings as it taxis, heading straight into the wind in order to get more lift. On a day with no breeze, the loon may be incapable of taking off, even on an empty stomach. Sometimes it will be stuck on a small lake for days until there is enough wind to permit takeoff on the short water runway.

No other bird has such a strong link to the past, and no other bird sings such a haunting wilderness lullaby. The Cree believed the loon's night cry was the lament of a dead warrior who was forbidden entry to heaven; the Chippewyans heard in it an augur of death. The loon has at least six different calls, each with its own message, among them a short hooting call, a "who" sound that serves to let the young know where the parents are, and a "gleea gleea gleea" warning proclaiming territory. Dan Gibson, a Toronto nature filmmaker, once put a decoy loon on the water; the loon claiming that bay as territory put his head forward and called out the challenge "gleea gleea." Then he dove, came up under the decoy, and flipped it over.

Springtime is also porcupine time. These animals are not aggressive, and when encountered will always attempt to leave the scene, either waddling off in an ungainly fashion, or climbing a tree, which they do with considerable ease. But when the hardwood forest is still naked of its leaves the porcupines have no protective cover. Only when a porcupine cannot escape a predator does it use its quills as weapons. Contrary to popular conception, these animals cannot throw any of their approximately 30,000 quills, but a swat from a porcupine's tail will dislodge several hundred sharp spines, and predators often die of infection from quill wounds. Only one animal (other than humans) can kill a porcupine—the fisher. This member of the weasel family will dart repeatedly at a porcupine's head, avoiding the tail, and inflict bite after bite until its victim is dead. Because fishers have been hunted for their luxuriant fur, they are virtually extinct in most of Ontario, and the population of porcupines in the province is unnaturally high. But in Algonquin Park the elusive fisher is protected, and the porcupine population remains at its natural level.

Frequently porcupines will invade a campsite at night to rummage among the cooking utensils. Then a great deal of snuffling and grunting can occur, and a camper may think the site has been invaded by an army of animals. More than likely it will be a porcupine scouting for a free meal. But there is always the possibility that the night visitor is a black bear.

By nature extremely shy of humans, some of the approximately 2000 bears in the park have been trained by careless campers to lose their fear of people, and they have become a nuisance at campsites. In the interior, bears have learned to scavenge when campers fail to hang all their food well off the ground at night; at car campgrounds, bears have been attracted

Porcupine

by careless disposal of food and by inadequate garbage collection.
Until the late 1970s, when park authorities increased their garbage collecting and began to educate campers on how to protect
their food, it was not uncommon for canoe trippers to lose all
their provisions to a marauding bear. And car campers often
spent wakeful nights listening to bears rattling the lids of garbage cans.

Fortunately, these incidents have become less frequent.

The bears of Algonquin Park subsist mainly on leaves in the
spring, and in the summer they devour the abundant raspberries,
blueberries and chokecherries. But there are still "garbage
bears" in the park, and once a bear has become a scavenger, it
will never go back to its wild ways. Feeding a bear, or leaving
garbage around for it to eat, amounts to signing its death
certificate. Scavenger bears are trapped by park rangers in large

45

culvert traps, tagged, and then released far from camping sites. But if a relocated bear returns to the site of its original scavenging it is shot, for it is impossible to rehabilitate a confirmed scavenger. Bears in the interior that have learned to go after people's food are also shot, for there is no way to transport large traps into the back country.

Although garbage bears are a serious nuisance, they are not dangerous. Since the creation of Algonquin Park there has been only one fatal incident involving a bear in the park: on 13 May 1978 three boys were killed by a male bear on a creek near Lake Traverse. According to the results of the autopsy, the animal was neither rabid nor starving; the killing remains a mystery, but such an event had never happened before nor has it happened since.

While the ice is melting from Algonquin's lakes in spring, the bears are beginning to wake from their winter's hibernation. Hunger probably awakens a bear; over the winter it loses as much as half its body weight. Hibernation not only permits the bear to live through the months when foraging would be impossible but it also allows the cubs to grow large enough to survive in the woods while they are still in the protection of the winter den.

Bears mate every second June, but the fertilized egg is not implanted until November. If implantation occurred immediately after fertilization (as it does with most warm-blooded species), the baby bears would be born in August, and their feeding requirements would interfere with the mother's autumn task of fattening up for winter. So the eggs wait until November to implant. They then take ten weeks to develop in the mother's womb. Two or three hairless cubs about the size of a chipmunk are born in January. For the rest of the winter the bear cubs stay awake and nurse while their mother sleeps. Sheltered by the warmth of their mother's body and safe in the den, they grow quickly. In early May the mother wakes and begins teaching her cubs to forage. But adult bears do not start to gain back the winter's lost weight until the poplar leaves on which they feed appear at the end of May. During that month, females must protect their offspring against adult male bears, which are at the point of starvation and will eat even their own cubs.

Another animal often encountered in Algonquin Park in

spring is the moose. Although moose do not attack humans, they are extremely dangerous on Highway 60 where they present a hazard to fast-moving cars. Along the highway, road crews have been spreading salt all winter. During spring thaw, salty puddles form, attracting moose, which are salt-starved after their meagre winter diet. Particularly at night, when their dark colour renders them almost invisible, they are dangerous to motorists. At least one driver has been killed in the park as a result of a collision with a moose, and many of these large animals die every spring after being hit.

And then there are the bugs.

In 1604 when the French explorer Samuel de Champlain paddled to within a few kilometres of the park, he wrote of "hosts of mosquitoes so thick they barely allowed us to draw breath, so greatly and severely did they persecute us." One hundred and fifty years ago a British woman named Anna Jameson wrote *Winter Studies and Summer Rambles in Canada* to document her travels in the colony. Of the spring she wrote: "Enough of mosquitoes I will never again do more than allude to them; only they are enough to make Philosophy go hang herself and Patience swear like a Turk or a trooper."

Expect mosquitoes from the beginning of June until the end of July, blackflies during the month of June only. Contrary to popular myth, mosquitoes do not die after one bite. Only the females attack, the blood of warm-blooded animals being required to develop their eggs. As the mosquito sucks up two or three milligrams of blood through a needle-like tube in its proboscis, it sends saliva back down the tube to dilate the blood vessel and keep the blood from coagulating. It is this saliva that causes itching. Blackflies inflict a far more painful bite. When you have been bitten by a blackfly, it helps to remember that a staple of this insect's diet is nectar from the blueberry flowers that bloom in the park in June. If there were no blackflies there would be no pollination and consequently no blueberries. Blackfly larvae are also an important food for trout. The ecosystem is an intricate web in which even the annoying bugs play an important role. Eliminating one member of it would have dire consequences for the entire system.

Blackflies lay their eggs in running water in fall. The larvae spend the winter under the ice, growing slowly. One square metre of stream can produce thirty thousand blackflies. When spring arrives, the larvae, wrapped in silken cases, change into adult blackflies under the water. The gas-filled cases, resembling tiny bubbles, rise to the surface and burst, releasing millions of young.

Both blackflies and mosquitoes are attracted to humans by the aura of warm, moist air that surrounds them. Repellent inhibits their biting by jamming their moisture sensors. In addition, these insects find certain colours unappealing, and people who wear bright colours, especially orange and yellow, will be less bothered by bugs.

It is wise to plan visits to the park with insects in mind. The month of May is perfect for both canoe tripping and hiking, though warm clothing and warm sleeping bags are essential. To one on foot in May, the hardwood forests have a lovely open feeling; the wildflowers are in bloom, and there are no bugs about. The canoe tripper will delight in both the absence of bugs and crowds in the interior. But visitors need to be cautious of spring water travel; in May the water is still very cold and therefore dangerous.

This is the season when the ice is leaving the park's lakes and rivers. After a winter spent under the mantle of ice, speckled trout, their sides glittering with flecks of scarlet and gold, rise to the surface to breathe in the oxygen-rich waters and to feed.

May and June are the prime months for fishing in the park. Speckled trout abound in the Nipissing River, lake trout and bass in lakes Opeongo, Laveille, Dickson, Big Crow, Cedar and others, and smallmouth bass can be caught in the Petawawa River. To find out which lakes are being stocked in a given year, contact the Ministry of Natural Resources, Box 219, Whitney, Ontario K0J 2M0. On the following lakes the use of motorboats of up to six horsepower are permitted, except during the months of July and August: Big Crow, Bonfield, Dickson, Hogan, la Muir, Laveille, Little Crow, Little Dickson, Proulx, Sundassa, White Partridge and Wright. A word of caution: it is not permitted to bring live bait fish into Algonquin Park.

For canoeists, the Petawawa River is one of the most exciting spring white water rivers in southern Ontario, but it should be run only by paddlers having advanced white water skills.

In June canoe tripping is still possible, but it is advisable to bring along plenty of bug repellent and avoid creeks and long portages. Campers will also be more comfortable on windy points and on big lakes during the fly season.

Following these precautions, one can spend time in the park as soon as the ice goes out; the rewards, in birdsong, luminous spring colours, and lack of crowds, are many.

Joanne Kates

Water-lily

*If I wanted to regiment society I'd first destroy the wilderness
so they wouldn't have any standards to judge it by.*

Wayland Drew

Summer

High summer is the season when Algonquin Park most closely resembles paradise. The hot sun finally penetrates the glacial rocks and the water is warm enough to invite endless swimming. Park visitors fish for bass in the shade of rocky overhangs and paddle through waters bright with strong summer sunlight. The warm nights encourage you to sit late around the campfire watching the moon rise and the stars crowd the sky. After midnight you may even be rewarded by luminescent streaks of northern lights on the horizon. By the beginning of July the blackflies are gone, and mosquitoes disappear by the end of the month.

In August the young of the spring's mating season make their appearance. A careful search of the ground will often reveal the entrance to a chipmunk's burrow and a glimpse of a den of baby chipmunks. On the waterways, flocks of ducklings and downy brown baby loons are shepherded by watchful parents. Moose calves graze with their mothers on swampy shorelines and bear cubs forage for blueberries and raspberries.

Summer is berry season in the park: first raspberries ripen in almost every open area from mid- to late July; next blueberries appear on sunny lakeshores from late July until mid-August. Two nonedible berries decorate the woods at this time of year: bunchberries, a bright scarlet aftermath of May's white flowers, and the large dark blue berries of the trout-lily, borne on tall stems and recognizable by their spiky leaves.

Few flowers continue to bloom in the dense shade of the hardwood forests or even in the coniferous woods except along trails where tree and brush cutting permits sunlight to reach the ground. One exquisite flower to look for in pine woods in early summer is the pink lady's slipper, a member of the orchid family; its delicate pouch-shaped bloom resembles an old-fashioned slipper.

The most abundant flowers in summer are found in the wetlands and clearings. The shore of every shallow creek is home to the tall purple-flowering spike of pickerelweed. Rarer is the cardinal flower, seen only on the banks of the Barron River and along the Petawawa River below Lake Traverse. This August bloomer turns riverbanks into a carnival of scarlet. On the edges of bogs, joe-pye-weed is a common sight in summer. Often growing two metres tall, it resembles yarrow but has dark pink sweet-scented flowers. An oddity is the pitcher plant, which inhabits bogs lacking the nitrogen it needs for its growth. Insects, attracted by the plant's nectar and reddish colour, crawl into the pitcher-shaped leaves, which are often filled with rainwater, then are unable to escape up the slippery sides past the downward-pointing hairs at the top. The insects drown and their nitrogen-filled bodies nurture the plant, thanks to nature's ingenuity.

The favourite flowers of canoeists, though, are the water-lilies, both the cup-shaped yellow ones and the magnificent white yellow-centred lilies. Bass hide in the shade of lily pads, the pads serve as patios for frogs, and moose graze on the whole plant.

The moose is North America's largest land animal, weighing up to 500 kg. In full antler, the male is an impressive beast. Although ungainly looking, a moose has no trouble running on its long legs through the woods at 60 km/h. But the male moose's glory are his antlers. Each April they begin to grow, nourished by a covering of velvet, a layer of hairy skin rich with blood vessels. By August the antlers are full grown and the animal rubs off the velvet against tree trunks. Now the bull is ready for the rut. In September bulls congregate in herds of two to five animals to establish the hierarchy that will determine which one has first choice of the eligible females. More than any other factor, antler size decides a male's place in the hierarchy. Violence is rarely necessary to establish position; posturing is usually enough.

Each bull mates exclusively with one cow for about a week

during mating season and, if he is high enough in the hierarchy, he will mate with a second cow and possibly even a third. By winter, the mating season over, his antlers fall off.

I saw my first moose in July 1966 on one of those paradisical days in summer: sun blazing Otterslide Creek into diamonds, pickerelweed studding the riverbank with amethysts. Swamp grass towered over our heads, creating the inner boundaries of a shimmering green world. Beyond the tall grass we could see cliffs dark green with pine trees, and above us white clouds raced across a bright blue sky. We came around a narrow hairpin turn in the creek and there he was, knee-deep in the water, making a lunch of water-lilies. He was a year-old bull with small velvet-covered antlers, and still slim enough to be graceful.

Moose were rare in the park then, but now there are an estimated 2800 of them, a doubling of their numbers in the past fifteen years. This increase is due to a decrease in the deer population. White-tailed deer carry a parasite which is not harmful to them but which is fatal to moose. The parasite, a worm, spends the first part of its life cycle inside the deer, then is excreted and spends the next stage of its life living off the snails and slugs that eat deer feces. Snails and slugs often cling to low vegetation, and when moose graze on leaves they unwittingly eat the infected slugs and snails as well. Unfortunately, the parasites do not pass through the moose but bury deep in its spinal column and eventually migrate to its brain. The animal begins to suffer from "moose disease," the symptom of which is aimless staggering, and it dies quickly thereafter. The disease is invariably fatal, and as long as Algonquin Park's deer population was high, few moose could survive there. Now that most of the deer are gone, moose are thriving.

Deer were not native to Algonquin Park, as were moose. These southern animals do not have the extremely long legs required to move through the deep snows of an Algonquin winter. Also, they feed mainly by browsing on the tender young shoots of shrubby trees like poplar, which were not common in the park before human intervention began to change the composition of its forests. But after the loggers arrived in the 1850s, the big pines were cleared away, removing some of the dense shade canopy. Accidents caused forest fires which created even more cleared area, and in these clearings shrubby growth took root. And so the deer moved in, attracted by the poplar browse. In winter they would "yard up" or congregate under stands of hemlock, which offered some protection from the snow. During the period when clear-cut logging was taking place, so much shrubby growth resulted that they could browse without having to break long trails through the snow. The arrival of the deer and their parasites spelled doom for the native moose. After the creation of the park, the area became even more hospitable to deer since they were protected from hunters within its boundaries. In the 1920s lodges opened and deer herds began coming to the lodge kitchens at night to be fed. The largest and most predictable herd was at Cache Lake; for several decades this herd appeared at the Highland Inn every evening for handouts. After Highway 60 was opened in 1936, deer quickly discovered that people in cars would stop and feed them.

The demise of the park deer began in the 1950s when many of the park lodges closed. In the 1960s Highway 60 was widened and straightened, reducing roadside browse. Logging companies began to cut timber more selectively; more big trees survived and shrubby growth was reduced. A combination of forest-fire prevention and the development of more efficient fire-fighting techniques vastly reduced the number of fires. As the park's forests gradually changed again, the deer population decreased.

No tame deer herds remain in the park today. The last time I saw deer there was just below Radiant Lake in 1981. I was canoeing with a friend down the Petawawa River. On the shore, anemones and tall purple gentians were blooming, and on the portages there were wild snapdragons and wild roses. As we paddled around a curve in the river, two white-tailed deer—a doe and a fawn—were browsing on the shore. We stilled our paddles, but these present-day animals will have nothing to do with humans. Off into the bush they bounded on light hooves, the dancers of the forest.

Summer is an ideal time to explore Algonquin Park. The two long park hiking trails are in perfect condition; car camping is possible in all nine organized campgrounds; canoe tripping is at its best; and the Highway 60 activities program is in full swing.

Fall ℞

The fall colours reach their peak during the last half of September, revealing the Algonquin Park of Tom Thomson. The colours are so dazzling, and Thomson's portrayal of them was so bold, that when he first brought his Algonquin canvasses home to Toronto, art patrons refused to believe he was painting real trees. Finally A.Y. Jackson came to the park one September and looked out across Canoe Lake at the flaming maple forest. "Yes, Tom," he confirmed, "what you're painting is really there."

At the beginning of September one solitary maple tree on a shoreline suddenly goes scarlet overnight. Then a birch high on a hillside turns yellow, and as September passes more and more trees turn, until the hills are ablaze with colour. The golden birches glitter in the sun; the poplars and beeches go yellow and orange. The oaks change later than the rest, into a deep, improbable burgundy. And the sugar maples become an unbelievably bright scarlet. The sight is magnificent in scale as well, for on the west side of the park where hardwoods are prevalent, the blazing hillsides stretch from horizon to horizon.

At the end of September, after the leaves fall, the hardwood forests still glitter, but now the scarlet and gold are underfoot. Although it is necessary to bundle up well against the cold autumn nights, September and October are beautiful months to visit the park, not only for the splendour of the foliage but also because the park is far less crowded than during the summer (with the exception of holiday weekends).

Sometimes a fall mist creeps in from the west and wraps the

Joanne Kates

How still it is here in the woods. The trees
Stand motionless, as if they did not dare
To stir, lest it should break the spell. The air
Hangs quiet as spaces in a marble frieze.

Archibald Lampman (Solitude)

forest in a pale grey cloud; canoeing through fog has an aura of mystery. It was on one such fall night that we were out for a late paddle. The lake was so still that the bow of the canoe sliced through it like a hot knife through butter, and the mist sat wet and shimmering on the water's surface. We could barely see the shore; above us was only mist, and even the birds on their way south were unseen, though we had heard them earlier. The one remaining pair of loons in the bay called to each other intermittently through the fog. Aside from that lonely sound, all was eerily quiet.

Suddenly a loud crack about three metres to our right nearly caused me to jump out of the canoe. It sounded as if someone had thrown a very large rock at us. I turned on the flashlight, and there in the water were two beady eyes, a pointed snout and a brown furry face. We had entered a beaver's territory and it had slapped its tail as a warning. Evidently our campsite was also inside that beaver's territory, for it continued to slap its tail most of the night while we tried to sleep.

We were on McIntosh Lake at a campsite ringed with aspens and alders, a favourite food of beavers. Fall is the season when campers are likely to run into these industrious animals; only then do they leave the security of their home ponds to gather their winter food supply.

For all Algonquin animals fall is an important period of transition. In winter, temperatures hover near 20 degrees below zero and summertime food sources are hidden under a thick mantle of snow. The park animals can be divided into four categories depending on how they get ready for winter: migrants (most birds); hibernators (such as bears), predators (wolves, otters) — the only animals to continue their normal food-hunting activities year round, and food storers (chipmunks, beavers). Because so many animals are foraging for winter food, autumn is a splendid time to see them in the park. If you go quietly, especially towards dusk, you will often be rewarded with glimpses of animals that are far more elusive in summer.

Beavers work at night to avoid being visible to predators, such as wolves, so the sight of a beaver is rare in the park; but beaver dams and lodges are impossible to miss for anyone who spends even a day paddling in the interior. There is approximately one beaver lodge for every square kilometre of park, and there are probably close to 5000 beaver colonies.

The dams—they can be as tall as 1 m and as long as 35 m —trap water upstream, creating a pond behind them deep enough not to freeze to the bottom in winter. The animals then build a lodge in the pond so as to have water access to it and to their food pile all winter, thus protecting them from predators. For their food pile, they cut down aspens and alders and drag them back to the home pond. There they pile them on top of one another until the huge mass sinks and only its top can be seen. After freeze-up beavers leave their lodges only to swim to their food pile.

Dam-building creates the right conditions for the production of the beavers' food. When they build a dam and create a pond, the trees upstream of the dam are killed and the pond becomes host to the tender aquatic vegetation— especially water-lilies—that beavers subsist on in summer. Although beaver engineering is intricate and seems so rational, researchers have demonstrated that all it takes is the sound of running water to stimulate the building instinct in this animal; they have placed beavers in tubs of still water and then played tapes of running water to them. Invariably, if suitable material is available, the animals will begin to build dams.

The beaver lodge is a complex architectural compound. It usually has two secret underwater entrances and several rooms inside. After the beavers have cut down trees (a sure clue to beaver work going on nearby is the sight of small stumps with the marks of recent gnawing), they drag the cut trees back to the pond, piling them up in the water and reinforcing them with mud. When the pile is about a metre above the water, they excavate a tunnel from below the water's surface up through the pile of logs to the water line. Just inside that entrance they build a feeding platform for winter meals, and above the platform they make a sleeping loft which they carpet with carefully shredded wood for soft bedding. They then plaster the outside of the lodge with a thick layer of mud which functions as insulation and also prevents predators from breaking in. The only uninsulated part is at the very top where they leave a breathing hole. An excellent self-guided tour of beaver technology, with a first-rate information leaflet, can be had at the Beaver Pond Trail (km 48).

Beavers are physically well suited for the work of dam- and lodge-building. They have special ear valves that close every time they dive underwater, and lips that close *behind* their front teeth so they can transport and work with wood without getting water in their mouths. Beaver teeth never stop growing and are self-sharpening. Their hind feet are webbed for swimming; a beaver can stay under water for as long as fifteen minutes and can swim submerged for as far as a kilometre. The beaver's tail is especially useful: it is a rudder for steering while swimming, a device for scaring away enemies (a loud slap on the water is a formidable noise), and a repository for the storage of fat to help the animal survive over the winter on lean rations. Fur trappers in the north consider beaver tail soup a great delicacy because of its fat content.

Beaver couples live together for many years; they mate once a year, in January or February, in the water under the ice. In May three or four kits are born, and they may not leave home until the following summer. Adult beavers often have to move because they invariably cut down trees faster than the trees can regenerate; thus as the years pass a beaver family has to range farther and farther from its lodge in order to cut enough suitable trees for the winter food pile. But such travelling increases the danger from predators such as wolves, so eventually the beavers leave the lodge and build another one in a new location. An abandoned lodge is easy to recognize because it has no food pile beside it; another clue is a dam that shows no signs of having received daily repairs.

When beavers leave a pond site, the unattended dam soon breaks; then the pond drains, and very slowly, over a number of years, the land returns to its natural forest state. The first stage of this transition is the beaver meadow—a lush, grassy area that results when the former pond dries up. The old dam is still in evidence, but the herons, ducks, otters and moose that frequented the pond are gone, for the aquatic food they subsist on is no longer available there. A fine example of a fairly recent beaver meadow can be seen approximately 500 m from Tom Thomson Lake on the portage to Ink Lake. The old dam (which is visible) is about 100 m long, one of the longest in the park. As the beaver meadow matures, trees take root there, first shrubby growth and eventually, years later, conifers and hardwoods. By then the cycle is complete: the beavers have caused a forest to change into a pond, then a meadow, and back into a forest again. The only other creatures that alter the land so completely are humans, and legend suggests we are related; the Sandy Lake Cree believed that beavers were once human but that evil befell them and they were turned into animals.

Sometimes a family of otters will move into an abandoned beaver lodge. The otter is even more proficient in the water than the beaver; it is the fastest-swimming mammal, able to outswim some fish. This streamlined brown weasel with whiskers on its face and webs between its toes is elusive, but otters can sometimes be seen in late fall when the young play with their mothers for the first time, sliding down muddy streambanks and sunning on rocks.

Ontario Ministry of Natural Resources

By October there is an urgency surrounding the activities of the animals that store food for winter, for their survival depends on how much food they can collect. This urgency makes them bold: chipmunks who chattered from the trees in summertime will come right into campsites in October and steal breakfast from a camper's plate. But the chipmunk's major autumn activity is finding hazelnuts and other nuts and seeds, stuffing them into its voluminous cheek pouches and scurrying back to the burrow to store them for winter. This burrow is an underground tunnel having separate food storage, sleeping, and toilet rooms. To conceal the tunnel's two entrances, chipmunks scatter the dirt from their excavations far enough away to mislead predators. Nonetheless, careful scrutiny of the ground will often reveal the 6-cm-wide holes. Throughout the winter these small rodents sleep in their burrows, waking only for meals.

While chipmunks are collecting food, bears are fattening themselves for their hibernation. They too are less elusive than usual now and can sometimes be seen in the interior feasting on beech nuts and other fall delicacies. Their scat is everywhere in the woods. By the time the animals have prepared themselves for winter, the world of Algonquin Park has turned from crimson to grey. Pine needles fall and scent the woods; loons' colours fade. The Algonquin lakes' water level drops as dams are opened to provide needed water downstream. This change exposes the rocky shorelines, creating a pale, desolate world. Overhead, flocks of honking geese pass on their way southwards. The leaves on the ground have faded, the hardwood trees are barren, and the lakes are starting to film with ice. In November the first snow falls, and by December the lakes freeze.

Because the park is at an altitude of 670 m, fall can be extremely cold; light frosts are not unusual in August and by the end of September heavy frosts are common. Winter comes so quickly to the park that nature hikes and other organized events cease after Labour Day, but some of the car campgrounds along Highway 60 stay open until Thanksgiving, as does the museum.

September is a superb month for canoe tripping: the interior is uncrowded, the fall colours are breathtaking, and with luck the days will be hot and sunny. The only hazards are cold nights and cold water. After the middle of September swimming is not advisable, and a spill in a canoe could easily result in hypothermia. In late September and throughout October hiking in the park may be the preferable activity, especially when the falling leaves create a magic carpet of scarlet and gold.

Joanne Kates

The silence so solemnly reigning,
And anciently patterned in wood,
Resembles the lines of a quatrain
To a princess asleep in a tomb.

Boris Pasternak (Hoarfrost)

Winter

Algonquin Park in winter is a frozen white expanse. The icy lakes and hillsides are covered in thick, sparkling snow; even the pine and spruce trees wear mantles of white. Few animals are visible, though many can be identified by their tracks in the snow. The only animals that pursue their normal activities during winter are the park's predators: the foxes, wolves and weasels. The otter, a member of the weasel family, exemplifies the life of a predator in winter. This animal's diet consists mainly of fish, frogs, crayfish and water bugs. In other seasons it simply slips into the water to hunt, but in winter it must search out places where streams are free of ice, then swim under the ice in search of its prey. The best places to see these aquatic hunters are near stumps rising from water, or on the downstream side of beaver dams.

Aside from the many animal tracks there is scant evidence of life in Algonquin Park in winter. It is the silence, and the vast white expanses of lake and woods where no creatures stir, that make winter in the park a special time. The few sounds seem magnified by virtue of the silence: the ice on the lake cracking and groaning like a prehistoric monster stirring in its sleep; the raucous song of a raven high overhead; the howl of a wolf.

Wolves are hunted for bounty in many parts of the world, but in Algonquin Park they are protected. Outside of the park wolves are rare, but it has not always been so. When whites first arrived in North America, wolves ranged from Mexico to the Arctic Circle; they lived in balance with their prey species and were not harmful to the native people. But during the eighteenth century, settlers from Europe were carving farms out of the North American wilderness, and this activity put them in direct competition with wolves. Settlers built fences around territories where wolves had been hunting for 10,000 years, and there they raised domestic animals. It was natural that the wolves would continue to hunt in their habitual range, and that they would then kill the domestic animals for food. Thus they earned the hatred and fear of humans.

On the humans' part this territorial competition had a psychological component as well. During the eighteenth century, the dawn of the industrial age, wilderness was seen as having an evil power that needed to be subdued by civilizing forces. Progress was equated with technology, which could be controlled, in contrast to wilderness, which was uncontrollable. For many, wolves came to symbolize wilderness, and what a perfect symbol they were: animals that emerged from the forest in the dark of winter's night, and made a wild, wild sound.

Throughout the history of literature—the seventeenth-century story of Little Red Riding Hood is a good example—wolves have been portrayed as dangerous to humans, but in fact the opposite is true. Wolves do not attack humans; on the other hand, humans have virtually wiped out wolves in Europe and the United States by poisoning them, trapping them and hunting them with guns. In 1793 Upper Canada's first parliament passed the Wolf Bounty Act, and the Ontario government paid a bounty to anyone who killed a wolf. (This bounty remained on the provincial law books until 1972.) Even in the new Algonquin Park the bounty was in effect; park rangers (who were poorly paid) earned extra money in winter by collecting wolf bounties, and fifty or sixty wolves were killed there each year.

If it were not for Douglas Pimlott, Algonquin Park would have lost its wolf population completely. Pimlott, the University of Toronto zoology professor who founded the Algonquin Wildlands League, dedicated his life to fighting the destruction of Canada's wild places and to defending wild animals against unjust persecution. From 1959 until 1965 he conducted a wolf research program in Algonquin Park; it was at his urging that the park dropped its wolf bounty when his study began. Pimlott found that there were approximately 150 wolves in the park in 1959. Some people feared that when the bounty was discontinued, the number of wolves would rise radically, but no such thing happened. Wolves instinctively limit their own numbers. The park's land mass can only support a certain number of wolves, and when humans stopped limiting their population, nature took over the task. Scientists do not know precisely how wolves keep their population down to a level the land can support, but experts hypothesize that one way is for a pack to cull excess pups. The majority of each season's pups do not survive the winter in the park because in the pack hierarchy they are the last to feed at a kill and often do not get enough to eat. It is also possible that the pack rejects some pups at birth.

Dr. D. Pimlott   Ontario Ministry of Natural Resources

Ravens are among the few birds that stay in the park all winter, and they are dependent for their winter sustenance on the meagre scraps left behind by wolves. When bounty money was still paid for wolves the raven came close to extinction in Algonquin Park because of the winter food shortage. Eagles also need the scraps from wolf kills for their survival during the cold winter months.

Since Pimlott's research ended in 1965, the number of wolves in the park has probably declined, because the number of deer, on which wolves depend for their food, has declined. But there is no truth in the charge that wolves are responsible for the decline in the deer population. The relationship between wolves and deer is the natural relationship between predator and prey in which wolves kill no more deer than they can eat, and their predation keeps the deer herd down to a level that the land can support. Without their natural predators, prey are no longer in balance with their land mass, and their survival is threatened. An example of what happens when a prey-predator relationship in the ecosystem goes out of balance occurred on the 145-ha Navy Island in the Niagara River where deer were introduced without any predators. The deer are multiplying too fast to be supported by the habitat and are in danger of starving to death.

Another element of the prey-predator balance between wolves and deer is the fact that wolves kill more old deer than those in their prime, and more sick than healthy deer. The reason for those choices is that wolves kill deer on the run, and it is only the old and infirm deer that cannot outrun a wolf. The exception to that rule occurs in summer when wolves do kill some fawns; in general, though, wolf predation helps to cull the less useful members of deer herds and therefore to ensure an adequate supply of food for those in their breeding prime—an important aspect of prey-predator balance.

If wolves were better able to prey on moose, their numbers would not be declining in the park, but it is extremely difficult for an animal the size of a large dog to bring down a 400-kg moose. Also, wolves are stimulated to chase an animal that runs, and moose will most often stand their ground when approached by wolves. In that case the wolves never attack. Even if the moose does run, bringing it down can never be accomplished by one wolf: a team effort is required. Wolves have always hunted deer by this method, often setting up an ambush. One wolf will hide on a lakeshore and three other members of the pack will drive the deer across the ice towards the first wolf.

In an attempt to survive the scarcity of deer, park wolves are beginning to prey on beaver. But beaver are only available in summer when they leave the water to cut down trees; during the winter they are protected by their strong-walled lodges.

Wolves live in packs that include one long-term mated couple and anywhere from two to six of their progeny from the past few years. The couple mates each spring, and nine weeks later five or six pups are born. Both parents spend the summer raising their family in a den; wolves' interpack social organization is so close that if a mother dies, another mother will adopt the pups and raise them. By fall, as soon as the pups are old enough to travel, the pack becomes migrant again, for their constant hunting over a large range necessitates a nomadic existence. Often two or more packs will meet at rendezvous spots, and winter visitors to the park may be lucky enough to find large clearings with the tracks of many wolves. From these clearings the packs will set off to hunt together for a while.

Wolves seldom fight among themselves. In order to settle disputes and to determine rank, they use elaborate rituals that clarify each animal's place in the pack hierarchy at any given moment. The two situations that particularly require this clarification are choosing mates and taking turns feeding at a kill. A senior wolf might put his ears forward and growl at a younger male. The young male will almost always put his ears back to signify his submission. If wolves are feeding and a young male is too greedy, the dominant male will snarl at him ferociously and perhaps even snap. The younger male will then flop on the ground and expose his belly—a message that he is willing to back off and wait till the leader has fed.

The only time that hierarchy does not prevail is when wolves howl; all the members of a pack howl together with no apparent leadership. Howling has several purposes: as a way of locating each other across kilometres of forest so that the pack can rendezvous after separating for a night's hunting; as a means for a lone wolf to locate its pack; and simply for the love of howling on nights when they are all together and the sky is clear. Wolves never howl when it is raining or heavily overcast; calm, clear nights are the best time to hear them.

When you hear wolves howl in Algonquin Park you are listening to some of the wildest music ever created. On a clear winter's night the stars set off sparkles on the broad expanses of snow; overhead the limbs of the spruce and pine wear heavy coats of white; the darkness and the silence are vast. To enter this magical frozen world, to raise your voice in a howl, and then to be answered by a wolf is to make contact with something ancient and wild both outside and within yourself.

In August the government runs public wolf howls on evenings when the park naturalists have located a pack. As many as a thousand people in a caravan of cars follow the naturalists along Highway 60 to a spot where the wolves were heard the night before. The naturalists howl and there is a fifty-fifty chance that the wolves will howl back. Experience has demonstrated that wolves will respond even to the poorest imitation of a howl. Information about the dates and times of public wolf howls is available at the park gates, the museum, and on bulletin boards at campgrounds.

Winter visitors to the park can try their voices at howling in hopes that they will receive an answer.

Most of the park's tourist facilities are closed during the winter. To get food, lodging and gasoline it is necessary to drive either to the town of Whitney (5 km east of the East Gate) or to Oxtongue Lake and Dwight (about 6 km west of the West Gate). Highway 60 is kept ploughed and sanded all winter, and there are groomed cross-country ski trails in the park as well as hiking trails suitable for snowshoeing. Snowmobiling is prohibited.

Algonquin Park becomes a true wilderness in winter; the temperature hovers at 20 degrees below zero (C and F) and the snow is at least a metre deep. Under those conditions a person can very quickly freeze to death in the out-of-doors. Anyone planning to spend time in the park in winter will need sophisticated winter equipment and clothing and advanced knowledge of how to cope with outdoor winter hazards. Because there are no rangers checking on visitors' safety, if you plan to spend time in the park you should advise a friend where you intend to go, when you expect to return, and ask that the police be notified if you fail to return. Particular caution is required when walking on ice; there are strong currents at creek mouths, and though the ice may look thick, it often does not freeze solid enough to support a person's weight.

During this season, park advice and information are available at the back door of the Park Museum (at km 20, measured from the West Gate) or at the East Gate (at km 55.8): Both these offices have detailed maps of all ski trails, and both are open every winter weekday from 8:00 A.M. until 4:00 P.M. The nearest doctor is in Whitney (705-637-2170) as is the nearest provincial police headquarters (705-637-2622 or Zenith 50000). There are pay telephones along Highway 60; the winter leaflet available at the East Gate and the museum indicates their location. Although snowmobiling and ice fishing are not permitted in the park, winter camping is. Only one Highway 60 campground is kept open all winter: at Mew Lake (km 30.6) where you will find a ploughed parking lot, free firewood (in the concrete block shed beside the parking lot) and an outhouse (but no electrical outlets). Once a day a ranger checks the parking lot, but campers should not rely on this service since provincial government cutbacks have rendered park services precarious.

CROSS-COUNTRY SKI TRAILS

There are 64 km of groomed, well-marked cross-country ski trails in Algonquin park. One of them, the **Old Track Ski Trail**, starts at the Mew Lake Campground and provides a 50-km round trip to Whitney and back along an abandoned railway bed. Three other approaches to the Old Track Ski Trail are at its Whitney end, at Rock Lake (8 km south of Highway 60 at km 40.3) and at the Pog Lake Campground (km 37). Except for the 18-km loop at the Whitney end of the trail, which is rated difficult, the Old Track is easy skiing.

The easiest ski trail in the park is the **Sunday Lake Trail** (km 40.3). It runs for 18 km on old logging roads, and halfway along the loop there is a rest area with a fireplace where you can cook lunch or make tea.

Ontario Ministry of Natural Resources

The **Leaf Lake Trail** (km 53.9, 2 km inside the East Gate) is designed for a range of skiing abilities; coloured markers indicate skill levels required. The Green Trail, for novices, is a 5-km loop; the Blue Trail, for intermediate skiers, is a 7-km round trip; the Black Trail, an 8-km loop, has steep hills (both up and down) and will appeal to advanced skiers. A rest area with a fireplace and firewood is centrally located so that all three loops pass it.

The only park trail designed for advanced skiers, the **Fern Lake Trail**, is a 13-km loop which starts at km 0, the West Gate.

Maps to all the ski trails are available free at each trail's entrance. The trail fee is $2 per day per vehicle, payable at honour fee stations at both East and West gates. Annual ski trail permits cost $10 and are available during office hours at the East Gate or the museum back entrance or by writing to the Ministry of Natural Resources, Box 219, Whitney, Ontario K0J 2M0. Skiers can also write to the ministry for trail maps and other information. Camping is not permitted on the ski trails.

Highway 60 Tourist Activities

Highway 60 runs for 55.8 km across Algonquin Park's southwest corner and is the only part of the park that has been heavily developed for tourist use. This corridor provides easy access to a variety of tourist attractions. To enter the park, visitors must pay a daily vehicle permit fee of $2.50 or buy an annual vehicle permit for $25. Activities along the corridor are held daily from the beginning of July until Labour Day and range from self-guided nature walks to evening slide talks in an outdoor theatre. The locations given for trails, campgrounds and other amenities all refer to their distance in kilometres from the West Gate. Information and brochures about park activities and services are available at both gates and at the Information Centre (km 23.3) or by writing to Ministry of Natural Resources, Box 219, Whitney, Ontario K0J 2M0.

There are three private lodges in Algonquin Park: Arowhon Pines at km 15.4; Bartlett Lodge on Cache Lake at km 23.3; Killarney Lodge at km 33.2. Reservations are suggested.

Nine beautiful lakeside campgrounds are: South Tea Campground West, km 10; Tea Lake Campground, km 11.4; Canisbay, km 23.1; Mew Lake, km 30.6; Two Rivers, km 31.8; Kearney, km 36.5; Whitefish Lake and Pog Lake, km 36.9; Rock Lake and Coon Lake, 40.3; Opeongo, km 46.3. The sites are suitable for car, tent and trailer camping. All have drinking water and toilets and some have showers but there are no electrical hook-ups; there is a trailer sanitation station located at km 35.6. Car campgrounds can also be found at Kiosk, Brent and Achray. Because of provin-

Recreational development is a job not of building roads into lovely country, but of building receptivity into the still unlovely human mind.

Aldo Leopold

cial park budget cuts, some campgrounds may be temporarily closed, so it is wise to check with the Information Centre before heading for a favourite site.

Along Highway 60 there are also picnic grounds, which are indicated by signs, and two stores: the Two Rivers Store at km 31.4, a small general store, and the Portage Store at km 14.1, a large complex which includes a general store, souvenir shop, restaurant, gas pumps and a complete canoe trip outfitter.

The Algonquin Park Museum (km 20.1) is interesting but small, and budget restrictions have prevented it from undertaking a much-needed expansion. Occasionally the museum runs children's programs. They (and all other Highway 60 activities) are listed in *The Raven,* the park's literate and informative weekly newsletter, which is published twelve times annually from April to September.

The park's other permanent exhibit is the Pioneer Logging Exhibit found just inside the East Gate at km 55.3. An audio-visual program shows the history of the park logging operations back to the 1830s, and a huge white pine log demonstrates the size of the trees in those days. There are logging sleighs and a lumber wagon, a replica of one of the old horse barns, a saddle-back locomotive and model of a camboose shanty, and even an alligator—a paddle-wheel boat that could winch itself overland across a portage.

But the park's major asset is its small but dedicated staff of naturalists who create the exhibits, cut the trails, lead the conducted hikes, and write the articles for *The Raven*. Every day from late June until Labour Day the naturalists lead day trips on foot or in canoes and present nature films and slide talks at the Pog Lake Outdoor Theatre (km 35.4) or, if it is raining, at the museum (km 20.1). During July and August they give daily camping and canoeing demonstrations and instruction, and in August they conduct public wolf howls for visitors in cars. Besides being listed in *The Raven,* these events and activities can be found in *This Week in Algonquin,* available free at all Highway 60 facilities.

There are also nine short self-guided walking trails and one longer trail, each of which illustrates a different aspect of Algonquin's nature. Trail guides are available for a small charge at the park gates or the entrance to each trail. Each one of the shorter walks takes approximately one hour, and all have numbered posts that correspond to the numbered information sections in the guides. The trails are:

Whiskey Rapids Trail (km 7.2)
This 2.1-km loop leads along the Oxtongue River to Whiskey Rapids —so named for the turn-of-the-century loggers who lost a keg of whiskey when they failed to see the rapids ahead. The keg was being delivered to the drive camp downstream, but the loggers dipped into it so many times they forgot about the fast water just around the corner. The trail guide discusses the ecology of an Algonquin river.

Hardwood Lookout Trail (km 14.2)

This 0.8-km trail reveals a typical Algonquin hardwood forest and includes a beautiful view of Smoke Lake and its maple hills. In autumn, the trail is at its best. The guidebook explains the ecology of a hardwood forest.

Peck Lake Trail (km 19.2)

This trail takes the hiker 2.4 km around Peck Lake, illuminating the life of the lake and its inhabitants.

Hemlock Bluff Trail (km 29.4)

This loop goes through 2.7 km of a typical Algonquin forest; the guide describes some of the animals that live in the area— moose, wolves, marten. There is a lookout with a fine view of Jack Lake.

Two Rivers Trail (km 32)

This 2-km trail is an easy climb to a cliff overlooking the Madawaska River. The guide explains some of the changes that have taken place in the park's forests.

Lookout Trail (km 41.8)

The trail, a 2-km loop, is the only rugged one of the interpretive trails. The reward for its steep climb is a magnificent view that encompasses hundreds of square kilometres of the park. The guide discusses park ecology.

Booth's Rock Trail (km 42.6)

J.R. Booth was the Ottawa Valley lumber baron who built the first railway through the park. This fairly strenuous 5.4-km trail visits the abandoned railroad, the ruins of an estate that belonged to one of Booth's relatives, and includes a spectacular lookout. The trail guide discusses the impact of humans on Algonquin Park.

Spruce Bog Boardwalk (km 45)

This 1.6-km walk winds through a typical northern spruce bog; the guide explains bog ecology.

Joanne Kates

Beaver Pond Trail (km 48)

This hilly 2.4-km trail takes the hiker past two beaver ponds, and the trail guide talks about the life cycle and habits of beavers.

Mizzy Lake Wildlife Viewing Trail (km 15)

This 11-km trail has the best wildlife viewing possibilities along Highway 60. It passes several inhabited beaver ponds and small lakes, and is home to beavers, otters, marten and moose.

In the Highway 60 corridor there are also seven children's summer camps. The first one—Northway Lodge for girls on Cache Lake—was built by an American in 1908. The second, Camp Pathfinder on Source Lake, is a boys' camp that was started in 1914, also by an American. Taylor Statten opened the first Canadian camp, on Canoe Lake, in 1921, and it was at Statten's Camp Ahmek that Pierre Trudeau learned to canoe. The first coeducational camp in the park was opened by Lillian Kates on Tepee Lake in 1932.

Joanne Kates

Two roads diverged in a wood and I –
I took the one less travelled by,
And that has made all the difference.

Robert Frost (The Road Not Taken)

Hiking the Park

The hiking trails of Algonquin Park are at their most splendid in fall when the forest is blazing with colour. Warm sleeping bags make it possible to camp until the end of October. Spring is also a favourite season for hiking the park from the time the ice goes out in late April until early June when the forest floor is a mass of wildflowers in bloom and there are as yet no bugs. But in a rainy spring the hiking trails are wet, so ankle-high hiking boots are essential.

Two trails have been designed for overnight use: the Highland Hiking Trail at km 31 and the Western Uplands Hiking Trail at km 3. The Highland Trail, developed in the early 1960s, has two loops, one of 19 km and one of 35 km; it is much used and its map is reliable. The Western Uplands Trail has three loops of 32, 55 and 71 km; it was developed in 1975–76 and the map currently in use was printed before its second and third loops were completed, so there are some discrepancies between map and trail. Some campsites marked on the map do not exist as of this writing. The rewards of the Western Uplands Trail, however, are substantial. It is less crowded than the Highland Trail, especially on the sections within one day's walk of the highway, and its campsites are easier to get to.

The first loop of each trail is the shortest and each successive loop is longer than the previous one.

Because use of the hiking trails is rising every year, there are not enough campsites on either trail, especially in the crowded sections near the highway. It is therefore wise to get an early morning start and set up camp early in the afternoon. Campsites are denoted by orange markers, and camping is permitted at designated sites only. No more than nine people may camp at one site, and anyone camping in the interior must buy an Interior Camping Permit for $4 per day per tent. Permits and hiking trail maps are available at the East or West gates or the Cache Lake Information Centre or by mail from Ministry of Natural Resources, Box 219, Whitney, Ontario K0J 2M0. The trail map costs 50 cents and is essential. A compass is not necessary.

When planning a hike, campers should assume that they will cover between 15 and 25 km per day. Using that estimate, it is wise to consult distances given for the various loops on the hiking map, and to choose an appropriate loop. Novice hikers out for a weekend will probably be comfortable hiking the first loop on the Western Uplands Trail or, given three days to hike, the second loop on the Highland Trail.

Most of the terrain on both trails is rugged and hilly. Although the hills are not difficult to climb and are certainly not dangerous, the rough terrain will quickly tire people who are not in good physical shape or are not accustomed to carrying a 20-kg backpack.

Like any other travel in the woods, hiking requires a respect for the future of the natural environment. Hikers should pack out all nonburnable garbage, leaving nothing behind but their footprints. In the absence of an outhouse the only way to avoid water pollution is to dig a privy at least 15 cm deep, a full 50 m from the water, and then to fill it in afterwards. Radios are not welcome in the silence of the wilderness.

All hikers should walk the trails in a clockwise direction, following the directional arrows on the trail map. There are two reasons for this rule: if everyone walks in the same direction, hiking parties will not encounter each other as frequently and their sense of privacy will increase; also, the trails have been laid out and signed with a clockwise direction in mind so it is much easier to get lost going counterclockwise.

Note: Map reference in text is to park trail map.

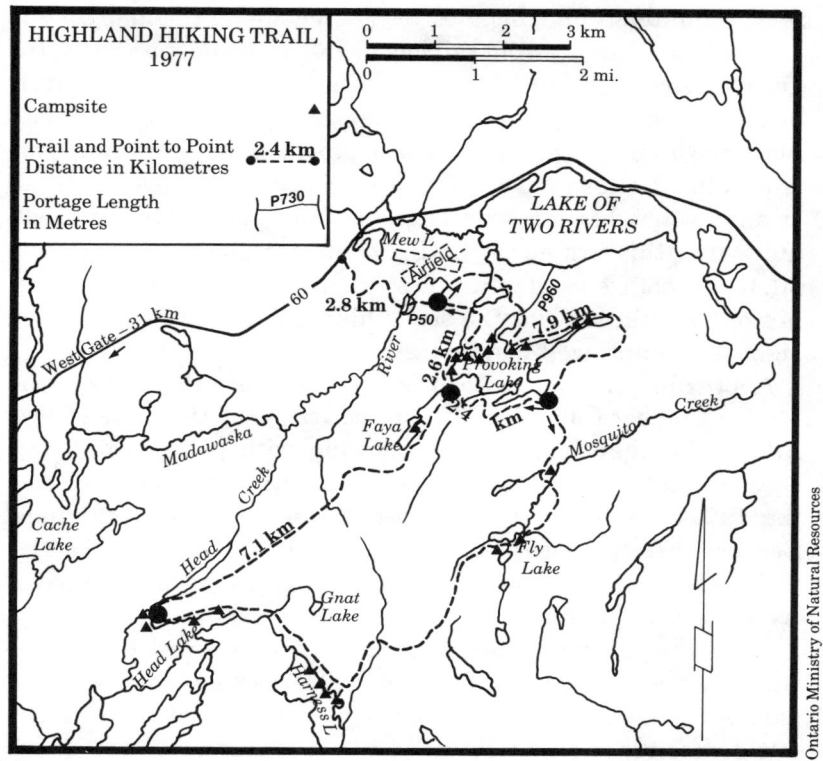

Ontario Ministry of Natural Resources

HIGHLAND HIKING TRAIL

First Loop: 19 km around Provoking Lake

The first steep hill comes in the first kilometre after the parking lot. At the top of that hill is a spectacular lookout over Mew Lake. Then the trail goes gently downhill, with a few steep pitches, to the Madawaska River, which hikers cross on a long wooden footbridge. Just above the bridge is a lovely small waterfall. Immediately past the river there is a very steep incline, but the footing is secure thanks to steps dug into the hill. At the top the reward is another magnificent lookout, this one with a view of Mew Lake and the old Lake of Two Rivers airfield. From the lookout to the first red dot on the map the walk is gently downhill.

At the intersection, denoted by the red dot on the map, hikers turn left and follow an old railway bed—the abandoned bed of the Ottawa, Arnprior and Parry Sound Railway, which was built by J.R. Booth in 1896 as a link in his logging empire. Neither ties nor rails remain and the old bed provides flat, easy walking. After almost one kilometre the railway bed rises to avoid a small swamp, which has a beaver dam and some open water. Immediately after this swamp the hiking trail veers to the right. Hikers often get confused and continue straight down the old rail trestle, but one should look for the small hiking sign which indicates a right turn onto a well-mowed trail.

Approximately 30 m after the right turn are the ruins of the McRae Lumber Company Mill on the left, near the Lake of Two Rivers. All that remains is a clearing with portions of a few derelict walls, but McRae's Mill was a thriving sawmill during the 1930s, having about twenty-five substantial log buildings. Because there is a clearing where the mill used to be, raspberries thrive here. Hikers passing by quietly in July have a chance of seeing bears feasting on the berries.

After the old mill site comes a steep climb which includes walking over a large, flat, bald rock. This rock face is an exposed part of the Canadian Shield; it is one of the oldest rocks in the world, possibly as old as a billion and a half years.

Now the trail climbs gradually to a lookout about 50 m above the shore of a small, nameless lake; visible are the Lake of Two Rivers airfield and most of Lake of Two Rivers. Descending from the lookout, you encounter another steep but short climb of approximately 30 m and then another easy descent.

At this point you need to avoid the confusion created by a number of spur trails that hikers have broken towards the campsites on the north shore of Provoking Lake, and also by a portage trail that crosses the hiking trail here. The main trail goes eastward along the north shore of Provoking Lake, passing four large lovely campsites. The first two are flat sites in hemlock groves; the second two have limited vistas because of the narrowness of the lake at its northeast point, but they are located in fine coniferous forest. However, Provoking Lake is a destination lake and attracts inordinate numbers of novice hikers who wish to avoid strenuous activity; their numbers and their tendency to camp in the same place for several nights creates crowding in these campsites. Furthermore, annoyances such as blaring radios are far more common on Provoking Lake than they are at campsites at a greater distance from the parking lot. Hikers who prefer a more peaceful and private experience would do well to put this lake behind them as quickly as possible. This first section of the trail is also crowded with day users from the Mew Lake campground.

After the trail passes the last campsite on the north shore of Provoking Lake, it veers southward past a beaver meadow on the left. The meadow is the result of a broken beaver dam which has dried up and returned to grassy vegetation, and is a prime spot to watch for browsing moose.

As the trail goes southwest towards the next intersection (indicated on the hiking map by a red dot) the coniferous forest gives way to magnificent mature hardwoods. In spring the wildflowers carpet the forest floor here and in the fall the trees are a mass of blazing colours.

The 2.4-km walk westward along the south shore of Provoking Lake takes the hiker up and down innumerable hills in a combination of hardwood forest and hemlock ridges.

At the next intersection (indicated on the map by a red dot) the sign tells the first-loop hiker to turn right towards Provoking Lake again. Hiking north along the east shore of the lake, the trail passes numerous campsites, all sheltered under a soft hemlock canopy and offering many flat tent sites. The two drawbacks to camping here are overcrowding and a plethora of shrubby growth at the lakeshore which makes swimming unpleasant. However, the fishing is excellent. Baiting one's hook with worms or green frogs caught at the lake is almost certain to attract bass.

On the north shore of Provoking Lake the trail turns northwest. The 2.6-km section from the lake to the old railway bed is almost all downhill. Near the small unnamed lake the pitch is very steep, but then becomes gradual again. After the railway bed you return to the parking lot along the 2.8-km trail where you began the hike.

Second Loop: 35 km around Head Lake

To begin the second loop, hike from the parking lot clockwise around Provoking Lake. At the southeast corner of the lake there is an intersection (indicated by a red dot on the map) where signs point you south for the second loop.

The trail goes gently downhill all the way to unimpressive Mosquito Creek. The terrain is moderately swampy and there are few lakes to camp on from the intersection where the second loop begins all the way to Harness Lake. The campsite on Mosquito Creek is buggy in summertime but is the only place to camp before Harness Lake. It would be wise to boil the murky water before using it for cooking or drinking.

The country from Mosquito Creek to Harness Lake is superb for moose-watching because of the tender aquatic plants that thrive in the swampy areas. Fly Lake is actually no more than a swamp covered with lily pads, which are the favourite summer diet of moose. On that section of the trail you will also see many spruce and balsam trees that have been killed by the spruce budworm, a less than cheerful sight.

The trail winds between two meadows shown as striped lake areas on the map, just south of Fly Lake. These are classic examples of the beaver meadow, a late stage in the life of a beaver pond. When the map was printed in 1977, there was a spectacular dam, over 3 m tall, located here; it burst just after the map was published, the water drained from the ponds, and meadow vegetation took over. As of this writing the meadows are covered in summer with metre-high luminous green grasses. Raspberries grow in this swampy section of the trail and in July when they ripen, the area is perfect for bear-watching.

Harness Lake has four excellent campsites, though the southernmost one has a steep, difficult drop from the site to the water. The other three are located in hemlock groves carpeted with soft hemlock needles and are open enough for good vistas. There are also flat rocks along the shore to swim from, as well as big rocks for reflecting the heat of campfires. This lake is superb for lake trout fishing, particularly in spring and early summer. Minnows caught right here on minnow hooks make the best bait.

The walk is easy north along Harness Lake through a lacy canopy of mature hemlock. A small bridge crosses Gnat Creek, which is sometimes flooded by beavers, so wet feet may be unavoidable. The trail runs close to the shoreline at Head Lake, and the campsites are located in groves of cedar, spruce and hemlock.

Although the fish in Head Lake are fewer than in Harness Lake, they are larger.

The trail veers northeast at Head Creek, passes an old logging dam, and follows a canoe route portage for a short distance. The nameless long thin pond is a beaver meadow, with a trickle of a stream running through it thanks to broken beaver dams. For the next 3 km the trail climbs relentlessly towards a lookout. The beginning, as the trail turns away from the pond, has a few steep hills, then the climb becomes gentler. Just before the lookout the trail crosses a nameless creek. The crossing is along a beaver dam where a 10-m section of the trail has been flooded, so it takes a bit of searching to find the trail again beyond the dam. The splendid view from the lookout encompasses Head Creek, the Madawaska River and a big swamp to the northwest, near the abandoned rail bed. You can often see moose grazing in the swamp.

Next the trail descends to a small swamp and then to Faya Lake, a beautiful, deep glacial hole. There is one glorious camp-site on a rocky point and, in the years when it is stocked, the lake produces an abundant population of speckled trout. After the trail climbs from the depression around Faya Lake it goes steadily downhill to Provoking Lake. At the Provoking Lake intersection the sign will indicate a left turn onto the final portion of the first loop which you follow back to the parking lot.

WESTERN UPLANDS
HIKING TRAIL 1977

▲ Campsite

●------2.4 km------● Trail and Point to Point
Distance in Kilometres

P730 Portage Length
in Metres

Ishkuday Lake
Islet Lake
Brown Lake
Weed L
10.9 km
Stammer Lake
14.9 Km
Loft Lake
Rainbow L
East End Lake
10.4 km
P4020
Otterpaw Creek
Pincher Lake
P270
P820 Terna
West Otterpaw Lake
Susan L
P820
Cashel L
Lark Lake
East River
10.9 km
P1220
Pincer Lake
Clara Lake
Lupus Lake
Redwing Lake
Lupus Creek
10.4 km
Thunder L
P1080
East River
Whitecat Lake
Norah Lake
Namakootchie Lake
8.8 km
Oak Lake
P690
P730
Dace Lake
Ramona Lake
Eu Lake
8.2 km
Maggie Lake
P1190
Guskewau Lake
Steeprise Lake
Leach Lake
Little Hardy Lake
Hardy Creek
Guskewau Creek
OXTONGUE RIVER
Maple Leaf Lake
15.4 km
60
Maple Leaf Creek

0 1 2 3 km
0 1 2 mi.

West Gate

Ontario Ministry of Natural Resources

WESTERN UPLANDS HIKING TRAIL

First Loop: 32 km to Maggie, Oak and Ramona lakes

Immediately after the parking lot the trail begins with a foot-bridge over the Oxtongue River. The water level fluctuates seasonally and with the weather; in the spring the river can be as much as 2 m higher than in the fall, and in a rainy spring there is water on the trail almost as far as the first intersection. At this fork hikers following the first loop turn left and climb a steep hill. After the hill the trail goes along a beautiful high ridge to a nameless creek. A short, steep hill leads down to the creek, which is easy to cross just below a beaver dam; after the crossing the trail goes uphill again. The next creek crossing—which has a picturesque small rapids—is also easy. From here to Maple Leaf Lake the terrain is rugged with many steep hills. Maple Leaf Lake has extremely clear water and numerous campsites in shady coniferous forest. A marked side trail leads to the campsites on the north shore.

Now a steady uphill climb leads to Leach Lake through majestic hardwoods. The trail approaches the lake from a high vantage point, an ideal luncheon stop but unsuitable for camping given the steep climb down to the lake for water. (On the way to Leach Lake the map indicates a campsite which, as of this writing, does not exist.)

From Leach Lake to Little Hardy Lake the trail goes steadily downhill, then crosses Hardy Creek at a very steep rock notch that has been carved by the water over hundreds of years. After the creek crossing, the walk is gradually uphill, through mature hardwood forest, to Steeprise Lake. Although there are campsites on Steeprise, they do not compare to the picturesque and spacious sites on nearby Maggie Lake. This gemlike lake has very clear turquoise water, reminiscent of a glacial lake in the Rocky Mountains, but the fishing is poor, as it is on most of the lakes along this trail. While walking along the east shore of Maggie Lake you should take care not to stray onto the portage trail, which is marked with yellow portage signs.

Approximately 1.5 km north of Maggie Lake there is a well-signed intersection where the first loop turns right. The first 35 m after the intersection are rough and rocky; the rocks make the footpath difficult to discern. The trail then goes through hard-wood forest, and just over 2 km after the intersection there is a side trail to the left that leads to Norah Lake. A new campsite has been developed on the eastern shore of this lake since the map was printed.

From the Norah Lake side trail turnoff all the way to Ramona Lake much of the trail follows abandoned logging roads. Oak Lake has two campsites which are neither attractive nor private since they coincide with the end of a portage trail. They are also small and hence have few good tent sites. From Oak Lake to Eu (pronounced "oo") Lake the hiking trail first goes south along the portage trail, then veers to the left. *This section is incorrectly shown on the hiking map.*

Eu Lake owed its water to the presence of a beaver dam, but during the late 1970s malicious canoeists destroyed the dam, and as a result the lake is almost dried up. Although it has a camp-site, the necessity of walking through 20 m of mud to get water should deter all but the most trail-weary hikers from camping there.

The trail from Eu Lake to Dace Lake begins with a few steep climbs and then goes downhill rather steeply to the lake. The single campsite here lies on low, rather wet land. From Dace Lake to the intersection (indicated by a red dot on the map) the trail climbs up a steep hill along an abandoned logging road. Just north of the intersection is an old logging landing where teams of horses used to drag timbers from the bush.

Directly south of the intersection the trail passes Ramona Lake, which has fine campsites. Fishing enthusiasts might take a side trip from here to Namakootchie Lake, which offers both lake and speckled trout. To get there, follow the side trail east of the main trail to the campsites on Ramona Lake, then follow the portage trail from the eastern tip of Ramona to Namakootchie. The fishing is best on the north shore of the lake where the water is deepest.

Back on the main trail, walking south from Ramona Lake hikers traverse a maple forest on an old logging road. About one kilometre south of Ramona, look for "bears' nests" in a stand of beech trees. Bears climb these trees in September when the beech nuts ripen, pull the limbs together into a tangle, and then

lie in the crotches of the trees feasting on the nuts. Even if there are no bears to be seen, the tangled branches are ample sign of their former presence, as are the permanent scars on the tree trunks from their claw marks.

The hike southward to Guskewau Lake is a lovely walk through gentle, rolling hills and beautiful hardwood forest. The fine campsite on Guskewau is located on a breezy point with big pine trees around it, and the lake contains speckled trout. Over half of the remaining section of the first loop follows overgrown old logging roads.

Second Loop: 55 km to Clara, Tern and Rainbow lakes

To begin the second loop, hike from the parking lot north to Maple Leaf Lake and then on to Maggie Lake. Approximately 1.5 km north of Maggie Lake there is a well-signed intersection where the second loop begins on a trail veering to the left. Immediately after crossing a nameless creek, the trail goes up a steep hill and then down again to low, wet land. It drops even lower as it crosses the East River to Whitecat Lake, actually a swampy, weedy bog. Now the trail goes through fairly gentle terrain to Samos Lake, which does not have the campsite indicated on the hiking map. On its neighbour to the north, Clara Lake, the two southernmost campsites shown do exist, but they are on the border of a rough old logging road and have limited flat space for tents.

From Clara to Cashel Lake is a very easy walk, but the campsites shown on Cashel do not exist as of this writing. Half a kilometre after the trail passes Cashel Lake there is a five-way intersection (indicated on the map by a red dot) which is well marked. Hikers following the second loop will walk east along the portage trail (marked with yellow portage markers) for approximately 150 m and then veer to the south to follow the shore of Pincher Lake. The Pincher Lake campsites marked on the map all exist and are lovely.

Both Tern Lake and West Otterpaw Lake have campsites that are marked on the map, but they are extremely rudimentary with little flat space and on mostly rough ground.

From West Otterpaw to Rainbow Lake the trail is fairly easy, having few big hills. From Rainbow south to Susan Lake the trail goes through mature hardwood forest and over rolling hills. Immediately after Susan Lake the trail climbs a very long, steep hill, steeper than any on either the Western Uplands or the Highland Hiking trails; its eventual reward is a stunning lookout over Susan Lake.

From here the walk to Redwing Lake is uneventful. To reach the campsites a 50-m climb down from the main trail is required. The first one has room for only one small tent; the second is somewhat larger and is sheltered by a hemlock grove; the third, though marked on the map, does not exist as of this writing.

After Redwing Lake the trail crosses Lupus Creek and then goes west to Lupus Lake, a deep glacial hole having very clear water and two campsites. The eastern one has a giant white pine tree at least a metre across, lying dead in the water. As you walk out on it to fill your water container, this tree is a reminder of the big pines that covered almost all of Algonquin Park 150 years ago before the loggers came.

Islet Lake trestle (Ottawa, Arnprior and Parry Sound Railway), 1896

From Lupus Lake the trail goes uphill to Thunder Lake and then along an overgrown logging road to Ramona Lake. At the Ramona Lake intersection (shown on the map by a red dot) the sign will indicate to take the left side of the fork and follow the final section of the first loop back to the parking lot.

Third Loop: 71 km to Islet, Brown and Rainbow lakes

To begin the third loop, hike from the parking lot north to Maggie Lake and then to Clara Lake and Cashel Lake. Half a kilometre after the trail passes Cashel there is a five-way intersection (indicated on the map by a red dot) which is well marked. The third loop begins here with the trail going north along the western shore of Pincher Lake. The campsites along this shore have adequate flat tent sites.

The walk from Pincher Lake to Weed Lake is very easy except

for one short steep hill just before Stammer Lake. The walk to Islet Lake—the most beautiful lake on this hike—is also easy. Here the campsites all have ample flat sites for tents, superb sunset views, and are situated so that western breezes keep the bugs away.

It is hard to believe that a century ago Islet Lake was an important transportation site with trains running every 20 minutes, day in and day out, across its north arm. Lumber baron J.R. Booth built the line in 1896 to consolidate his transportation interests and to provide transport for his logs to market; the line also carried grain from the west, and when World War I broke out, it was used to carry troops. There were armed guards stationed at every trestle to prevent enemy sabotage, and one of those trestles—a massive log bridge—was at Islet Lake. The rail line no longer exists and the trestle has been filled in with earth, but viewing it is still worth the side trip of less than half an hour from the main trail. Hikers should leave the main trail where the map shows a red dot and hike north along the shore of Islet Lake towards the rail line. There is no footpath and it is essential to keep close to the shore while bushwhacking in order not to get lost in the dense undergrowth.

Returning to the main trail, the walk from Islet Lake to Ishkuday Lake follows a beautiful hemlock ridge. The path underfoot is soft and springy with needles, one of the delightful features of the Western Uplands Trail, which has not yet been overused.

From Ishkuday Lake to Brown Lake the trail passes through some very rough country and climbs several extremely steep hills as well as crossing many overgrown logging roads.

The hike from Brown Lake to Loft Lake is uneventful, easy and pretty. Halfway between the two lakes there are two campsites marked on East End Lake which do not exist as of this writing, nor does the campsite marked on the small unnamed lake one kilometre east of East End Lake. On Loft Lake there are three campsites marked on the map but only the northernmost one has been built. From Loft Lake it is an easy hike to Rainbow Lake. At the Rainbow Lake intersection (shown by a red dot on the map) the sign will indicate to turn left and follow the final sections of the second and then the first loop back to the parking lot.

Six Selected Canoe Routes

Canoe tripping seems to put people in closer touch with nature than any other outdoor activity. The very physical effort required to reach the crystal lakes of the park's interior makes their beauty appear more precious. At first it is the silence one notices—the only sound the gentle music of paddle pulling water. While the ears rest, the eyes feast on landscapes that would remain unrevealed except by courtesy of the canoe. Hours spent paddling the enchanting park waters, a dinner prepared in the open, the quiet drama of the sun slipping down behind a ridge of pine trees while loons call to each other, a night canopy of stars— this is surely the equivalent to spending a few days in paradise.

This chapter is a guide to that paradise. It is not, however, a lesson on how to manage a canoe trip. Canoe tripping involves potentially dangerous situations; careless campers have drowned, injured themselves seriously with axes, or become lost and died of overexposure. Novices should make their first canoe trip with competent, canoe tripping friends or with one of the several groups that organize canoe expeditions. Some of these groups are noted on page 153, and a number of books on how to canoe trip can be found in the reading list on pages 155-56. The books contain useful information, but they are no substitute for first-hand experience with a good teacher.

To canoe trip in Algonquin Park, there are three requirements. All canoe trippers must carry one life jacket for each person, and must buy an interior camping permit, which costs $4 per day per canoe. You also need a canoe routes map, which costs $1.00. Both permit and map can be bought at any canoe trip access point; the

Joanne Kates

Can you put a bit to the lunging wind?
Can you hold wild horses by the hair?
Then have no hope to harness the energy here.
It gallops the wind away.
But here are crooked nerves made straight.

Douglas Le Pan (Canoe-Trip)

map is also available at either park gate or by mail from Ministry of Natural Resources, Box 219, Whitney, Ontario K0J 2M0. The map, which is to a scale of 1:126,720, shows campsites, marked with red triangles, and portages, marked with the letter "P." It is the only guide needed to travel the park by canoe. (The maps reproduced in this book are for general reference only.) Topographical maps and compasses are superfluous; it is possible to reckon by comparing the lake and land conformations shown on the map with those you see on the shorelines. Along the routes, portages are designated by large yellow signs and campsites by large orange signs. Both types of sign are easily located and are visible from more than half a kilometre away. There are approximately 1200 campsites in the interior of the park; most have outhouses and fire grills.

More than 70,000 people canoe in Algonquin Park every summer; 70,000 people can seriously damage a fragile wilderness, and they do. The government has set up canoe tripping rules to protect the park from becoming an exurban garbage dump and to minimize the impact that people have on its fragile ecology. Cans and bottles are not permitted in the interior. No more than nine people may camp on one campsite together. Camping is not permitted anywhere but at marked campsites. Campers must carry out all garbage that they do not burn. On certain lakes, which are close to access points and therefore in danger of being overused, you may not camp for more than one night.

Since the early 1970s, when those rules were made, the general deportment of canoe trippers in the park has improved. There are no longer large piles of rusting cans and broken bottles at every campsite. Nevertheless the rules are routinely broken, and the consequences to the environment are severe. Every portage trail and every campsite is still littered with garbage that campers have failed to pack out. People continue to camp on sites where no camping is permitted. On lakes like Joe Lake, where camping is permitted for one night only, hundreds of people stay for a weekend or longer. Especially on the lakes near access points, canoeists paddle in with radios and coolers full of beer. The beer is against the rules, and the radios should be, for sound travels extremely far over water and a blaring radio is incompatible with a wilderness experience.

In Algonquin, enforcement of the rules would require teams of rangers on constant patrol throughout the park and more thorough checking of canoeists when they buy their permits, as is already being done in some U.S. parks. Many people feel that such procedures threaten the freedom of their wilderness experience. But if the rules are not soon enforced, there will be no wilderness in which to be free, for it will have vanished under a pile of garbage. Because Algonquin Park is such a heavily used recreational area, it needs to be protected by careful management. But the government has put a low priority on park management. Although the total budget for the Ministry of Natural Resources has tripled in the last decade, parks spending has remained almost constant; thus, taking inflation into account, the park department's budget has been dropping by approximately nine percent every year. The employees who run Algonquin Park are both dedicated and talented, but there is a limit to their ability to maintain its facilities on a shrinking budget. In 1975 there were fifty-six rangers working in the interior of the park to clean up the campsites, maintain the portages, and make sure that people were obeying rules; in 1982 there were eighteen. Portages and campsites are not being cleaned. Canoe-trippers are not being monitored, and so they are breaking the rules. If the most recent budget cuts are not rescinded, services will deteriorate even further.

When choosing a route for a canoe trip, campers would be wise to bear in mind that the beer-and-garbage-style of canoe tripping is most prevalent on lakes near access points. One long portage usually separates canoe trippers from the unwelcome noise and debris common to these points.

There are twenty-nine points of access to the park's 1600-km canoe route network and each one leads to a trip of a slightly different character. Each also has its daily quota of canoeists; however, the quotas have been set so high that they are rarely filled except on holiday weekends. Fifty percent of the quota spaces for each access point may be reserved in advance by writing to Ministry of Natural Resources.

The access points along Highway 60 lead to the most crowded routes. A cause of overcrowding at the Canoe Lake access is the unusually high quota of canoeists—presently 125 groups—permitted to leave this point daily. Another drawback here is the glut of canoe trippers leaving this area as a result of the Portage Store, which provides a complete outfitting service and rents hundreds of canoes. Also along the highway lakes you will find a high concentration of cottages and motorboats.

On the other hand, choosing an access point in the northern section of the park requires a longer drive from southern Ontario, sometimes along mediocre dirt roads. To reach Achray, on the east side of the park, for instance, involves a seven-hour drive from Toronto. But the rewards after arriving at these obscure access points are quiet, privacy and the availability of campsites.

There are many good loop canoe routes, which allow campers to begin and end at the same access point without retracing their steps. But there are also some magnificent one-way trips, such as a run down the Petawawa River, for which it is necessary either to organize cars and drivers so that there will be cars at both the start and finish points, or to rely on hitchhiking from the end point of the trip back to your car. In summertime, it is usually possible to "thumb" a ride in the park.

Only one part of Algonquin Park is not popular for canoe tripping: the so-called "panhandle"—the townships of Bruton and Clyde in the extreme south. This area is full of small lakes and long portages, giving it the least desirable canoe tripping configuration.

It is important to remember that canoe routes change from year to year and indeed from week to week. Water levels rise and fall substantially, depending both on rainfall and on adjustments to water flow through the twenty-seven adjustable dams in the park. A creek may be a small torrent in May, with rapids to shoot; two months later the water level could be low enough that you may need to drag your canoe through it or portage around it. What took five minutes to paddle in the spring may take three hours to drag in the fall. Portages change too. Although cutbacks have forced park staff to reduce maintenance, they choose to maintain the heavily used portages and campsites. A camper may slip and slide on derelict catwalks on a portage in July, then return in August to find strong new ones.

The chart on pages 96-97 gives the salient points of the park's

MAJOR CANOE ROUTE FEATURES

	TRIP #1 Canoe L. to Big Trout L. to McIntosh L.	TRIP #2: Canoe L. to L. Louisa to Cache L.	TRIP #3: Achray to Barron Canyon	TRIP #4: North Tea L. to Nipissing R. to Cedar L.	TRIP #5: Opeongo L. to Crow R. to Laveille L. to Dickson L.	TRIP #6: Cedar L. to Petawawa R. to McManus L.
Access Point	Canoe Lake	Canoe Lake	Achray Station	Round (Kawawaymog) Lake	Opeongo Lake	Cedar Lake (Brent)
Degree of Crowding	Very Crowded	Crowded	Not Crowded	Not Crowded	Not Crowded	Deserted from Brent to Lake Traverse; crowded from there to McManus Lake
Degree of Difficulty	Very Easy	Very Easy	Easy	Moderately Difficult	Difficult	Difficult
Portage Difficulty	Very Easy	Easy	Easy	Difficult	Difficult: includes a 5305-m portage	Very Difficult
Canoeing Skills Required	Novice	Novice	Novice	Ability to manoeuvre in tight river turns	Expert: big lakes which are dangerous when windy	Expert, with at least intermediate white water skills
White Water or Flat Water	Flat Water	Flat Water	Flat Water	Flat water	Flat Water	Flat water and white water
Wildlife	Some: moose in Otterslides	Very little	Look for moose	Abundant, especially moose and waterfowl	Abundant	Abundant, especially moose and waterfowl

	TRIP #1: Canoe L. to Big Trout L. to McIntosh L.	TRIP #2: Canoe L. to L. Louisa to Cache L.	TRIP #3: Achray to Barron Canyon	TRIP #4: North Tea to Nipissing R. to Cedar L.	TRIP #5: Opeongo L. to Crow. R. to Laveille L. to Dickson L.	TRIP #6: Cedar L. to Petawawa R. to McManus
Lakes or Rivers	80% lakes 20% rivers	Lakes	Small lakes	70% rivers 30% lakes	70% lakes 30% rivers	River
Unspoiled or Developed	Somewhat developed	Many cottages and motorboats	Unspoiled	Unspoiled	Unspoiled	Unspoiled, except for Lake Traverse
Historical Sites	Abundant	Few	Very few	Several	Several	Abundant: Site of major Algonquin log drives from 1850 to 1945
Scenery	Lovely	Not spectacular except for Lake Louisa	Magnificent Barron Canyon	Beautiful narrow river, Nipissing R.	Magnificent big lakes; huge virgin pines in two locations	Magnificent river with a spectacular canyon, The Natch. The park's best scenery
Campsites	Abundant	Sufficient	Sufficient	Barely sufficient	Abundant	Abundant before Lake Traverse. Barely sufficient from Lake Traverse to McManus Lake
Circuit or One Way	Circuit	Circuit	Circuit	One way	Circuit	One way
Length of Trip	5 days, but can be shortened	5 or 6 days, but can be shortened	Weekend: 2 or 3 days	10 days, but can be shortened	5 days but can be shortened	10 days, but can be shortened to 4 or 5 days by beginning at Lake Traverse

major canoe routes. Most of the trips listed on the chart take five days or longer, but all lend themselves to being partly done. A brief look at the Canoe Routes map will show how any of these trips can be abbreviated to fit into a long weekend. For example, Trip #6 down the Petawawa River will take ten days, but starting at Lake Traverse instead of at Brent would make it a lovely four days of river running; Trip #5 is a taxing five-day circuit, but campers could start at Opeongo Lake and paddle to Big Crow Lake for a weekend's fishing. The possibilities are numerous.

In general, the west side of the park is more rewarding in autumn because it has more hardwood forest and hence more colour. Spring and early summer are the best times to choose routes that involve a lot of creek paddling since when the water is high it is unnecessary to drag canoes. The Canoe Lake to Burnt Island Lake corridor is an easy weekend trip in spring and fall but will be very crowded in summer. During insect season (June and July) camping is best on big lakes where wind keeps bugs away. Trips #1, #2 and #3 do not include any fishing lakes of note, but Trips #4, #5 and #6 offer superb fishing on both lakes and rivers.

A city dweller may think that once you've seen one pine tree, you've seen them all, but Algonquin Park's topography and forest cover vary enormously from one area to the next, and this variety is the reward for the canoe tripper who tries a different corner of the park every season.

Canoe Routes: Trip #1

Canoe Lake—Big Trout Circuit

Park habitués call this route Main Street, and for good reason since it is the most crowded canoe route in Algonquin Park. Ironically, it is also the only major canoe route inside the 8.9 percent of the park that has been set aside as a primitive zone, and no logging is permitted here.

There are fifty-two cottages and two children's camps on Canoe Lake, and Joe Lake has cottages as well. Tepee Lake has a children's camp and Little Joe Lake has a lodge. Motorboats are permitted on all these lakes. The disadvantages of this route include competing for campsites and being distracted by the sound of motors and noisy canoe trippers; the advantage is its proximity to Toronto—only a three-hour drive away.

This five-day trip, which can easily be shortened into a weekend excursion, begins at the Canoe Lake access point. The route leads north along Canoe Lake past three islands in the middle of the lake, then passes a large bay on the left. Immediately after the bay a big point extends into the lake on the left. Only crumbling foundations and some stone chimneys are visible on it now, but from 1872 until 1897 the boom town of Mowat was located here. It included the Gilmour Lumber Mills (its ruins can be seen on the shore), boarding houses and shacks for the workers, a mill hospital, a school, a stable for the fifty horses that made up the mill's team, and 700 residents. There was a Presbyterian missionary and a Roman Catholic priest who came regularly to save the souls of the men who worked there and to baptize their

Leon Muszynski

The movement of a canoe is like a reed in the wind.
Silence is part of it, and the sounds of lapping water,
bird songs, and wind in the trees. It is part of the medium
through which it floats, the sky, the water, the shores.

Sigurd Olson (The Singing Wilderness)

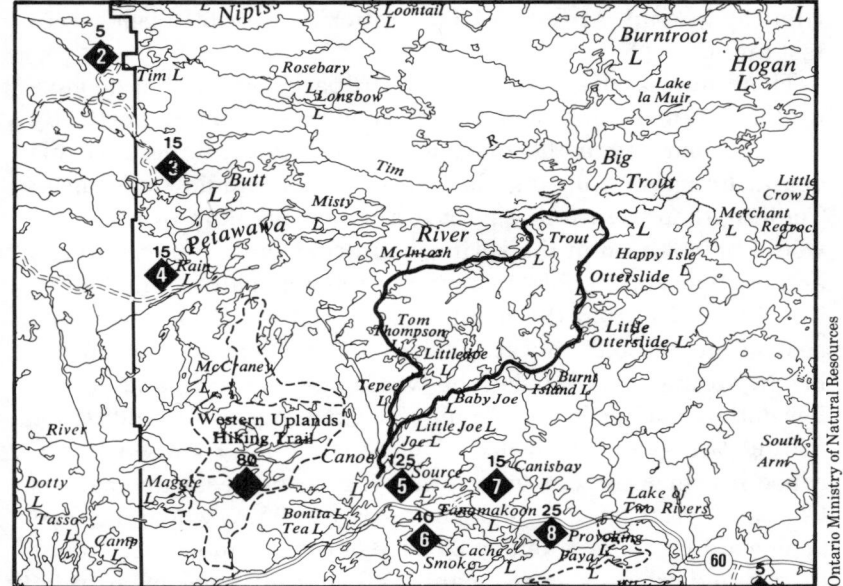

Canoe Trip #1

babies. In 1897 the pay at the mill was $1.50 a day; in 1900 the company went bankrupt as a result of the depressed timber market. The mill closed, the workers and their families left, and Mowat became a ghost town.

Shannon Fraser had been the Mowat postmaster, and he stayed on after the mill closed. In 1931 he and his family refurbished one of the old boarding houses and opened it as a fishing resort, naming it Mowat Lodge. One of Fraser's first guests was Tom Thomson, a young graphic designer from Toronto.

Thomson fell in love with the brazen spring and fall colours of the Algonquin forests. He spent a good part of the summer of 1913 on Canoe Lake, and back in Toronto that winter, he enticed his friends with tales of the park's spectacular colours. The following summer there was a real artists' colony at Mowat Lodge. Tom Thomson came back bringing A.Y. Jackson, Frederick Varley and Arthur Lismer. By fall their sketches were propped against every available wall of the lodge. In a letter to a friend that year Thomson wrote: "You don't notice the cold a bit. All you notice is your breath dropping down and splintering on the scin-

101

tillating ground. At Canoe Lake Station it was 45[F] below zero last night."

Thomson was so enchanted with the park colours that he gave up his job in the city in order to spend more time up north. By 1915 he had begun the routine that was to continue until his death: he painted during the winter at the Studio Building in Toronto, then went to the park in time for breakup in April. He would paint through the spring, capturing the luminous greens and icy blues of the forest coming to life. (He painted his haunting *Spring Ice* from the point directly across the channel—due east—from the old Mowat townsite.) Come summer, when the bright spring colours faded, he would stop painting and earn a few dollars doing odd jobs—a bit of fire ranging, some guiding for fishing trips—and a good deal of scrounging. Thomson had a canoe in which he took great pride, a graceful cedar and canvas Chestnut craft of a unique dove-grey colour, which he had achieved by adding a deluxe $2 tube of cobalt blue artists' paint to a standard grey canoe paint. When the frosts of autumn started turning the leaves crimson and orange, Thomson would take to his canoe again and spend every waking moment until freeze-up capturing those colours on canvas.

His paintings were, for Arthur Lismer, "the spirit of Canada made manifest in a picture." They are not pretty, but they are breathtaking; they speak of the power and energy of the north country, and of its rugged beauty.

While Thomson was paddling his canoe all over Algonquin Park in search of new vistas to paint, Mowat Lodge was his base and Canoe Lake was his home. On 8 July 1917 he set out from the lake to go fishing, his other passion next to painting. Before getting into his canoe that day, he joked with a friend about trying to catch a giant trout that had been eluding both of them. That was the last time anybody saw Tom Thomson alive.

Martin Bletcher, an American who was staying at his parents' cottage on Canoe Lake, saw an overturned canoe that afternoon but neglected to report it until the next day. On 10 July another Canoe Lake cottager found Thomson's canoe floating upside down on the lake. And on 16 July, eight days after he disappeared, Thomson's partly decomposed body was found in the lake. There was a four-inch bruise on his temple, and a copper fishing

Tom Thomson at Tea Lake dam, c.1913

line was wrapped around his left ankle sixteen or seventeen times.

Thomson's sorrowing friends buried him in the tiny Canoe Lake cemetery, about one kilometre west of Mowat Lodge, up from the shore. But his family lived in Leith, near Owen Sound, and they wanted Tom to rest there, so they quickly arranged to have the body moved. The next night an undertaker arrived at Canoe Lake on the train. Shannon Fraser offered his help in the exhumation, but the undertaker preferred to work alone and asked only that Fraser show him where the grave was.

The man worked by himself from 9:00 P.M. until midnight, during which time he allegedly dug up the body, put it into a metal casket, and soldered the casket shut. The next morning Fraser brought his stagecoach to the cemetery to fetch the new casket; as he said afterwards, when he helped lift it onto the coach he thought it seemed too light to be holding a body. Mark Robinson, the local park ranger, had been a great friend of Tom Thomson's and, being curious, he went to the cemetery that day to look at the undertaker's handiwork. His opinion was that the undertaker had not dug a hole big enough to take out a casket.

The new casket was taken to Leith and buried in the Thomson family graveyard. Meanwhile the Canoe Lake summer community discussed the mysterious death at length. Thomson was an expert canoeist and swimmer, and his death made no sense to them. How did he get the bruise on his temple? And why did Martin Bletcher (now dead) not report the dumped canoe the day he saw it? Everyone on the lake knew Thomson's canoe; and dumped, deserted canoes were a rarity. Martin Bletcher was known as a heavy drinker with a fierce temper that got worse when he drank. And he lived in the cottage next to Winnie Trainor and her family (on the west side of Canoe Lake, near Mowat). People say that Winnie and Tom were secretly engaged. He certainly did spend a great deal of time with her in the summers and visited her in the winters. Winnie Trainor never married, and when she died in 1962 she left a great many Tom Thomson sketches. Her nephew, who has seen her private papers, says that she and Thomson had made plans to marry in August of 1917.

Martin Bletcher was sweet on Winnie Trainor too; furthermore

104

he had never liked Thomson. World World I was in progress and Bletcher was an American draft dodger of German extraction. Thomson was a patriotic Canadian who, according to some sources, tried several times to enlist but had been turned down because of flat feet. The night before he disappeared, Thomson baited Bletcher for deserting the American army, and the two men quarrelled bitterly.

The questions surrounding Thomson's death have never been answered. His artist friends were so upset that they stopped coming to Algonquin Park. In a letter of 4 August 1917, A.Y. Jackson wrote: "Without Tom the north country seems a desolation of bush and rock. He was the guide, the interpreter, and we the guests partaking of his hospitality so generously given."

Thomson's artist friends designed and built a Canoe Lake memorial to him—a rock cairn with an inscription—on a hill just above his favourite campsite. To find it, paddle across the channel east from the old Mowat townsite to the tip of the big point at the north end of Canoe Lake. To the right of a small dock is a path that climbs up the hill about 25 m. The inscription reads in part:

He lived humbly but passionately, with the wilderness—it made him brother to all untamed things of nature. It drew him apart and revealed itself wonderfully to him . . . .

The mystery of Thomson's death remained unsolved, and in 1956 a longtime Canoe Lake summer resident, Judge William Little, organized an expedition to investigate the grave. The group found the old Canoe Lake cemetery and began digging at the point where Thomson had been buried. On that spot they dug up a coffin with a skeleton in it, confirming their long-held belief that the undertaker had never exhumed the body. When an anthropologist examined the skeleton and said it was that of an Indian, Judge Little and his cohorts refused to accept that opinion. They returned the skull to its original grave and marked it with a small wooden cross. Judge Little subsequently wrote a book, *The Tom Thomson Mystery*; one of the arguments he put forward to support his contention that Thomson's body never left Canoe Lake is the peculiar behaviour of Winnie Trainor after Thomson's death. She continued to spend summers at Canoe

Lake, a lonely and embittered woman who visited the cemetery frequently, always removing any flowers that had been put on the grave. If Thomson's body was not resting there, asked Judge Little's book, then why was Winnie Trainor so possessive about the gravesite?

Mowat Lodge is gone. It burned to the ground in 1930, and Shannon Fraser left Canoe Lake for good.

North of the Tom Thomson cairn, Canoe Lake branches into two channels. The left channel leads into Potter Creek, which offers an interesting historical side trip. On the left-hand shore is an old brown cottage, once owned by Gilmour Mills and used in the late 1800s as the checkpoint for all supplies arriving at the mill and lumber leaving it. North of the house is a wooden bridge across Potter Creek; it too is a remnant of Canoe Lake's bustling past, having served as a highway for teams of horses hauling logs to the Omanique Mill during the 1930s. Parts of this mill's foundations remain.

The right channel leads north towards the Joe Lake portage. The 295-m portage, which is more of a road than a path, can be shortened by paddling upstream to the right of the portage marker and landing at the first clearing on the left. At the end is a large clearing, the site of an early logging camp.

A channel leads from the portage out into Joe Lake. Just before the railway bridge at the end of the channel there is a hill on the left shore. In 1905 the splendid Algonquin Hotel was built on that hill overlooking the lake. Visitors would take the train from Toronto to spend their summer vacations there, taking advantage of the fishing guides provided by the hotel. In 1936 a room in the Algonquin Hotel cost $16 per week including full board and lodging. But during the 1950s the railway was phased out and the hotel became unnecessary. In 1957 the government dismantled and burned it.

The route leads north along Joe Lake, to the right of Joe Island. As early as the nineteenth century, European travellers were aware of this lake: in 1829 Alexander Shirreff, one of the first white men to travel through Algonquin Park, recorded in his journal that Joe Lake was "very picturesque." On the right shore of the lake, opposite the first campsite on Joe Island, is a camping spot at the site of a 1920s lumber mill—Jameson's Mill.

It burned to the ground after operating for only a year, and many stone and iron remnants remain at the location. A lucky camper might pick up an old logging boom chain as a souvenir of the park's great logging era.

From Joe Lake the route goes into Little Joe Lake. Then there are two easy portages of 435 m and 200 m, having a short paddle between them. On the first portage it is possible to wade through the creek and drag canoes instead of portaging, but this manoeuvre involves lifting canoes over a small log chute. After the second portage there is a small lake, then a narrows where fallen trees must be avoided, and then the channel opens magnificently into Burnt Island Lake.

This lake is big and beautiful, but it can be very windy; wise canoeists arrange to paddle it in the morning before the wind awakens. Just as soon as the lake widens from the narrows, campers who paddle to the shoreline on the right have the opportunity to look for the remnants of Minnesing Lodge, another railway hotel. Find the small clearing just before the first campsite on that right-hand shore. Land at the clearing and follow the old path uphill approximately 50 m to the three tall stone chimneys lined in a row.

Minnesing was built to attract visitors to Canada's wilderness. In January of 1913 several railway officials, guided by park ranger Mark Robinson, snowshoed to Burnt Island Lake to choose a site, and the hotel was built that summer. Minnesing, a glorious log building, did a roaring business. Guests had a choice of how to reach it: they could take the democrat, a horse-drawn taxi, over 16 km of extremely rough road from the Cache Lake train station; or, if they were wealthy enough, they could hire guides and canoes at Cache Lake and be chauffered there via Joe Lake.

In 1923 Dr. Henry B. Sherman of Carmel, California, bought the lodge. Having decided to dedicate his life to spreading the gospels, he turned Minnesing into a gospel school. The Minnesing school sent missionaries all over North America, Europe and the Far East until the early 1940s when it closed. Now all that remains are the stone chimneys and the crumbled foundations.

Burnt Island Lake has an abundance of beautiful campsites, but they suffer the same problems as those on Joe Lake: overuse

Former Camp Minnesing, Burnt Island Lake

has depleted the supply of burnable wood and has also caused the sites to be littered with garbage. The two finest sites on the lake are both on islands. The second island on the way down the lake (opposite the first point on the right) has a lovely campsite on the end that faces Joe Lake; there are two good tent sites and excellent rock ledges for swimming, sunbathing and sunset-watching. The other fine island site is Caroline Island, which has a big fireplace and panoramic lake views from both ends of the island.

After Burnt Island Lake on the way to the Otterslides, there is a 790-m portage that resembles a road and has hardwood chips underfoot for comfort. Just before the portage the Trout Lake ranger tower is barely visible on the horizon to the left. At the end of the portage look for a giant runner from an old logging sled, which was used to drag logs through the winter forest to the rivers for the spring drive downstream.

The two Otterslide lakes both have many beautiful campsites to choose from. There is a particularly fine one to the immediate right of the 540-m portage heading north. Even if you are not ready to camp, it is advisable to break here for lunch because the next few hours will be spent in creek country, which is pictur-esque but too swampy and buggy for stopping. Furthermore, there is no place to camp between the Otterslides and Big Trout Lake, so it is not advisable to leave Otterslide after 1:00 P.M.

This section of the route has a magical quality. The grass along the creek banks grows higher than canoeists' heads; hawks wheel in the sky, and there is a chance of seeing otters, moose, ducks, mink and great blue herons. During a rainy period the por-tages—which come in quick succession—may be muddy, but they are flat and easy to manoeuvre.

On the cliff to the right, just before the portage, peregrine falcons used to nest. The peregrine falcon is the fastest animal on earth; it cruises at 110 km/h and when it dives to catch its winged prey, it is moving at 250 km/h. These birds were once common everywhere in the world except Antarctica. In medieval Europe they were prized by royal falconers and were trained to hunt from the hand, as they still are today in Arab countries. But during the 1950s peregrines began to disappear, first from Europe and then from North America. The DDT they were ingesting was causing them to lay eggs having shells so thin that they would crack before the young could hatch. By 1969 the spraying of DDT was banned in most of Canada, but it was too late: the majority of the peregrines were already gone.

As with the loon, spending the summer nesting period in Algonquin Park did not protect the peregrine falcon from envi-ronmental poisons. Peregrines live by eating other birds—such as redwing blackbirds—which they catch on the wing. The red-wing winters in, say, Tennessee, where it feeds on insects that eat sprayed farm crops, or perhaps sprayed corn in a crib. The redwing blackbird can tolerate the amount of insecticide that it picks up from insects during its lifetime. But if at age five it gets eaten by a falcon and the next day the falcon eats another black-bird with its load of poison, eventually the falcon will have ingested so much poison that it is no longer healthy enough to reproduce. This problem affects all predators at the top of the food chain and is the source of their endangered status.

The government is trying to reintroduce falcons to Algonquin Park. Since 1977 they have raised fifty-four peregrines on cliffs above Hogan and White Trout lakes, hoping that at least some of the birds will survive and perhaps even return to the park to nest. Researchers in Alberta hatch the chicks; when they are one month old they are sent east on Air Canada flights. Algonquin Park gets six or eight chicks every spring, which they raise in boxes placed high on the cliffs. The chicks are fed quails through tubes in the boxes rather than directly by humans, so that they will not become tame, for their survival depends on their ability to hunt as birds of prey. When the chicks are approximately six weeks old the doors to their cages are left open, though quails are still dropped down the feeding tubes. Then, during the summer of their adolescence, the young falcons come and go as they please, instinctively learning to fly and to hunt. You can see them wheeling and diving as they chase shorebirds, climbing towards the sun, then dropping like bullets.

Every year since the program began, the young falcons have left the park in August, as peregrines always did. So far none has returned to nest in the park, and none has been seen nesting anywhere else.

After the peregrine cliff there is a 730-m portage, a short creek paddle and then a 105-m portage. A path leads to a waterfall near the end of the second portage. On a hot day this is a lovely cool place for a drink and a snack. Next an approximately fifteen-minute paddle leads through a narrows to Big Trout Lake.

Big Trout is an intensely dark blue lake having many splendid campsites. But it can be very windy and is also an easy lake to get lost on, so it is important to watch the map carefully here. The island campsites all have fine views, though it will be necessary to paddle to the mainland to find firewood. Because Big Trout is such a big lake, noise is rarely a problem as it is on Joe Lake.

On the first long point to the right after the entrance to Big Trout, there are three lovely campsites. The two easternmost have sandy beaches that extend far into the lake. The extreme easternmost site, however, requires climbing a sand cliff. All these sites have glorious views and the appropriate orientation for sunset-watching. There is also a delightful group of campsites on the last big point on the right (between the words "Big" and "Trout" on the canoe routes map).

It takes most campers one or two days to paddle from Canoe

Lake to Big Trout Lake. In 1932 Omer and Jim Stringer paddled from Canoe Lake to Brent (on Cedar Lake) and back in twenty-four hours. They covered the distance from Canoe Lake to Big Trout in less than five hours. Their gear consisted of only a few chocolate bars; they took turns carrying their canoe, and ran every portage.

Omer Stringer was born in 1912 to one of the first Algonquin Park rangers. He can still carry his canoe faster and farther than most people half his age. Omer spent the early part of his childhood at Brent and the later part at Canoe Lake. His teenage summers were spent as an apprentice fishing guide and his winters working as a logger. Starting in the 1930s Omer began working during the summer at various children's camps in the park, and has taught generations of children how to paddle canoes as well as to build and repair them, how to carve paddles out of black cherry wood, and how to live in the woods.

When Omer Stringer and I took our first canoe trip together, I expected to eat lukewarm meals and sleep on the hard ground. I thought camping was synonymous with physical discomfort. Omer insisted on cooking dinner that first night. He produced piping hot steak, potatoes and vegetables, miraculously all ready at the same time. Afterwards there was good brewed coffee and a chocolate cake baked on his reflector oven. We slept on soft brush beds (nowadays they would be foam pads). And breakfast was as sumptuous as dinner had been. I was confused. "Omer," I asked, "are you sure this is roughing it?" He replied: "It doesn't take an expert to be uncomfortable. Why should you suffer because you're in the woods?"

After Big Trout Lake the route leads through Trout Lake. Just before the lake's end, on the left, there is a ranger cabin in a clearing, indicated on the map by a tiny black dot. If the day is clear it is worth the trouble to hike to the old fire tower. The walk, up a very steep hill along a well-cut path, takes approximately an hour and a half; your destination is a metal tower on a cliff, with an octagonal cabin on top of the tower. The ladder has protective rings on it and is not dangerous to climb, but it does sway disconcertingly in the breeze. The tower is no longer in use—the park now depends on airplanes for forest-fire detection—but there is still a log book to sign in the cabin. The view is breathtaking; on a clear day you can see almost to Canoe Lake. Beside the tower there is a path leading to a ledge, from which you have a hawk's-eye view of Grassy Bay.

After Trout Lake the route leads through Grassy Bay, another magical creek paddle with tall grass and a few beaver dams over which you must lift your canoe. Although Grassy Bay is a labyrinth, there are luminous markers on stumps to prevent campers from getting lost.

Next come two portages into McIntosh Lake, first one of 745 m and then a 510-m one. McIntosh Creek, which flows between these two portages, is narrow and shallow and seems to go on forever. When the water is low it will be necessary to get out of the canoe and drag it. Canoeists must watch for the many underwater rocks here.

McIntosh Lake is a favourite of park old-timers. All of the campsites on the southeastern points have superlative lake views; when the sun sets, shadows dance on the water and the trees on the other side of the lake sparkle with the light's reflection. Of the campsites on the western shore, which are also excellent, the second one from the southern end of the lake has a tent site right on the water.

The route leaves McIntosh Lake via an unnamed creek heading south. The creek is narrow and winding; its shores are lined with pitcher plants and other bog flora and the straight trunks of tamarack trees, rare for Algonquin Park. Their pale green feathery foliage stands out against the cliffs covered with darker green fir, cedar and pine.

The creek leads into Ink Lake, a small, unattractive body of water, and then to the infamous 1700-m-long Ink Lake portage. This portage acquired its bad reputation during the 1970s when it included more than 25 m of derelict and terrifying catwalks and one hollow with sides so steep that it was almost impossible for a person wearing a pack to climb it. But Ink Lake no longer deserves its negative image, for the catwalks have been completely repaired, the hollow has been smoothed out, and steps have been cut into the hill. It is now a moderate portage, a bit hilly but with no impossible sections. After approximately 1200 m the portage trail turns out of the forest to cross a meadow.

Until the late 1970s the trail skirted this meadow, which was then a swamp. The old trail is still visible, but campers should not be misled by it; there are yellow portage signs at the beginning and end of the meadow indicating the path across it.

This terrain is an excellent example of the latter stage of beaver pond ecology. Beavers dammed the small stream above the meadow and it was a pond for a number of years. When the food supply in the area was exhausted, the beavers abandoned the pond; without its daily repairs the dam burst and water drained from the pond, leaving a swamp. The broken dam, which was one of the longest beaver dams in Algonquin Park, is still visible; the path through the meadow leads over it. During the 1970s the swamp slowly dried up; by the year 2000 it will be forest again.

At the end of Ink Lake portage is shining Tom Thomson Lake, a breezy lake having many campsites. It is not wise to try to find a campsite any closer to Canoe Lake, because there will be competition for the best sites. It takes less than three hours to paddle from Tom Thomson back to Canoe Lake via Tepee Lake.

Joanne Kates

If there is magic on this planet, it is contained in water.

Loren Eisely

Canoe Routes: Trip #2

Canoe Lake – Porcupine – Louisa Circuit

To do this entire trip in a leisurely fashion requires five days, but part of the trip could be made in a three-day weekend by paddling from the access point at Cache Lake south to Lake Louisa and back. Whether campers choose to do part or all of this trip, it has the virtue of being accessible from Highway 60, and thus a short drive from Toronto. But you must expect to find cottages and crowds of canoe trippers, and it shares with Trip #1 the motorboat problem as well. However, Lake Louisa, the focus of this route, has neither motorboats nor cottages, and its high, rocky campsites invite you to contemplate the Canadian Shield's fierce beauty.

The full trip begins at the Canoe Lake access point, initially heading south through the Canoe Lake narrows to an easy 355-m portage into Smoke Lake.

Smoke Lake has more cottages than any other lake in Algonquin Park; motorboats of unlimited horsepower and waterskiing are allowed on it, and camping is not permitted. Fortunately the lake is so large that the boats and cottages are not unduly distracting. The noise and environmental pollution produced by waterskiing are not consistent with a natural environment, and I believe the sport should be banned on the eleven park lakes where it is permitted.

Smoke Lake is a fairly long paddle, particularly if the wind is coming from the north. Halfway down the lake, on the point north of Molly's Island, Nominigan Camp stood until the late 1970s. Like Minnesing on Burnt Island Lake, Nominigan was a lodge built by the Grand Trunk Railway to promote tourism in the Canadian wilderness. It opened in 1913 but fell into disuse during the era of car camping and was finally dismantled, a regrettable decision, for the log building was a splendid relic of Canada's history.

At the south end of Smoke Lake there is a 240-m portage into Ragged Lake. Near the beginning of the portage, the trail splits into two branches. The left branch is a moderately easy walk up a steep but not impossibly difficult hill. The right branch is known as the Devil's Staircase. Although this trail is shorter than the other one it is far steeper; for every 1 m forward it goes up almost 2 m and sure footing is required. On the left side of the portage campers will see an old log flume that was used for sliding logs downstream from Ragged Lake into Smoke Lake. Water once raged through the flume, but now it has completely dried up.

Ragged Lake is easy to paddle, and the 590-m portage into Big Porcupine Lake is equally easy. This delightful lake has sparkling blue water and many good campsites. One of the most attractive is located on the point of land that juts far out into the lake, extending westward and almost cutting the lake in half. Of the point's four campsites, the best is the second one from the south; it is situated high on a cliff but is protected from the wind and has an ideal perch for watching sunsets.

It is not necessary to make the 395-m portage from one arm of Big Porcupine to the other; simply paddle around the lake, through the lovely shadowed narrows and into its southern section. After that a 370-m portage takes you into uninspiring Little Coon Lake.

From Little Coon to Lake Louisa the route includes almost as much portaging as paddling. The first two portages, of 895 m and 430 m, are separated only by a nearly dry pond. McGarvey Lake is the last place to get drinking water until Lake Louisa.

The 810-m portage leaving McGarvey Lake presents no problems, but Lemon Lake is no more than a swampy little beaver pond; its water is just a metre deep in some spots. The paddling and portaging from Lemon Lake to Lake Louisa is an utterly forgettable prelude to the most beautiful lake south of Highway 60 and one of the most beautiful lakes in Algonquin Park. The campsites are situated on high ground and have excellent views;

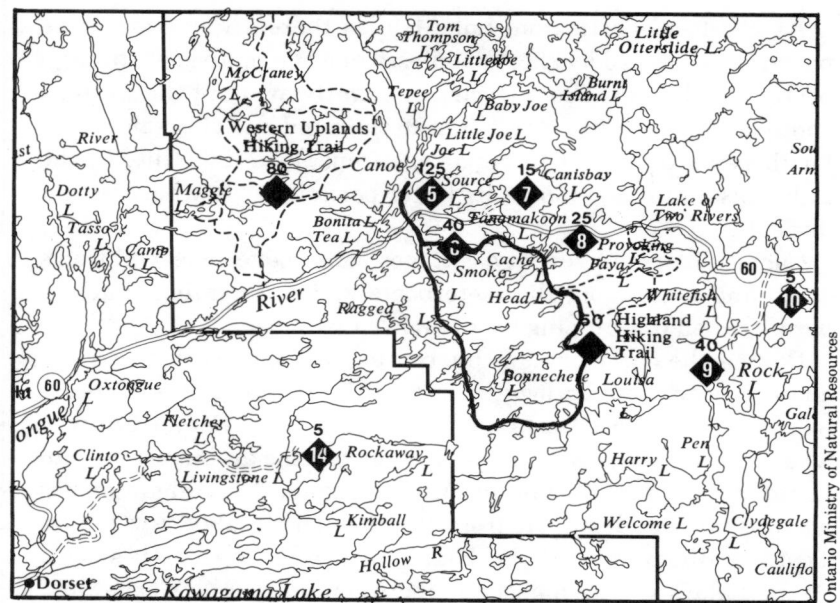

Ontario Ministry of Natural Resources

Canoe Trip #2

below on the shore are fine beaches. My favourite site is on the easternmost island, just before the lake starts to narrow towards Louisa Creek (between the words "Lake" and "Louisa" on the map). The height of this island provides campers with a superlative vista. Those interested in early history might search along the lake's north shore at its eastern end for smudged ochre pictographs, which were painted on the rocks by Indians several thousand years ago; however, they are extremely difficult to find.

Louisa is a lake of haunting beauty, especially in early summer when the new growing tips on spruce and fir shine luminously and the bunchberries are in gentle white bloom. But acid rain has caused dangerously high levels of mercury to be released in this lake and the big trout are no longer fit for human consumption. Campers wishing to fish in Lake Louisa should consult the Ministry of Natural Resources to find out which fish they can safely eat. To observe the effects of logging on the Algonquin forest, campers can explore the north or south shore of the lake 100 m back from the shoreline. These areas were extensively logged between 1975 and 1981.

117

As you head north from Lake Louisa there are five moderate portages separated by short paddles. Then the route goes through pretty Head Lake. The fine campsite on the point of the western shore is elevated but protected from the wind and offers flat spots for three tents. The 1640-m portage from Head Lake into Cache Lake has a hilly section on its latter portion but is otherwise not difficult.

Cache Lake has seventy cottages, one lodge, one children's camp and noise from the motorboats and waterskiing that are permitted on it. Camping is not allowed.

During the early part of this century Algonquin Park experienced a boom both in logging and in the building of wilderness lodges. When the Ottawa, Arnprior and Parry Sound Railway was built in 1897, Cache Lake Station became an important hub in the park. Guests bound for Minnesing and Nominigan lodges would take the democrat from the Station. In 1908 the Grand Trunk Railway opened the Highland Inn on the north side of Cache Lake's southernmost bay (between the words "Cache" and "Lake" on the canoe routes map). It was an elegant hotel that had accommodations for 150 guests, a billiard room, tennis courts and a formal ballroom; dressing for dinner was compulsory. But when the highway came through Algonquin Park in 1936, rail travel began to diminish and the old railway hotels lost their following. In 1957 the Highland Inn was dismantled and burned, and the next year the railway made its last commercial run through the park. As with the other railway hotels, the demolishing of the log building is a historical loss.

The route leaves Cache Lake via a narrow, romantically leafy channel which leads into Tanamakoon Lake where there is a children's camp and where motorboats of unlimited horsepower are permitted. Next a series of short hops, by paddle and portage, lead into Kootchie Lake, more of a mudhole than a body of water.

The 835-m portage from Kootchie Lake into Smoke Lake is extremely steep at its beginning and is muddy after heavy rain. However, in 200 m it levels out. From here it takes one hour to paddle to the Canoe Lake access point.

Canoe Routes: Trip #3

The Barron Canyon

Canoe trippers on the Petawawa River and in the area of Grand Lake will be rewarded with the sight of oak trees, which are rare in the western part of the park. The hills that guard the Barron River are rich with these dowager oaks, and in autumn, their deep burgundy leaves hang on long after the maples and birches have let the wind steal their scarlet and gold. Oaks make a significant contribution in the fall by providing bears with calorie-rich acorns for food. Unlike chipmunks, which build elaborate subterranean burrows for the winter, bears are cavalier about where they spend their hibernation period. They build no den but simply pull together branches and leaves under a pile of brush, a tree trunk or a rock overhang. With little external insulation, the bear depends solely on the sustaining power of the calories it has taken in during its period of autumn fattening, and on its thick winter pelt.

Trip #3 begins at the Achray Station access point, which is, as of this writing, difficult to find. Although the Algonquin Park canoe routes map is otherwise superb, occasionally it gives only sparse information for locating access points. Some of these points, like Achray, are off the beaten track, and the map directions for finding them are inadequate. To get to Achray, leave Pembroke on Highway 17 and turn left at a crossroads where a sign indicates a right-hand turn towards Pembroke Airport. Then turn right on the first road you come to and follow it to Achray—altogether about a seven-hour trip from Toronto. The

The Barron Canyon

Oaks don't drop their leaves
as elms and lindens do.
. . . .
Leaves hang on withering
tougher than leather
Wind tears them loose.
. . . .
When frost crispens the morning,
they give up nothing willingly.

Marge Piercy (The Doughty Oaks)

120

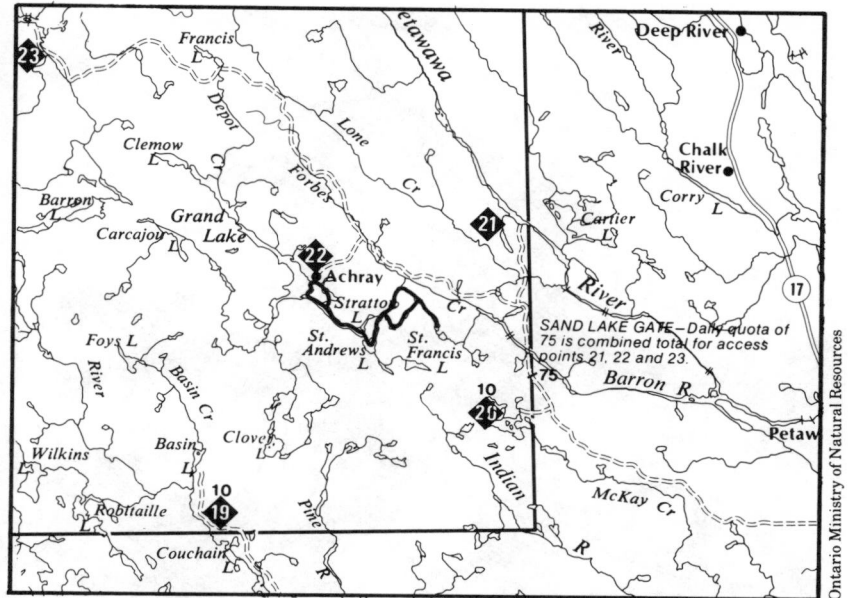

Canoe Trip #3

Barron Canyon can be an ideal three-day weekend trip if you stay the night at a motel in Pembroke. You can then be on the water early in the morning of day one. The easiest route involves paddling south to St. Andrew's Lake and setting up camp there that night. You can then make the canyon a full day trip on the second day, leaving day three for your return.

On Grand Lake motorboats are limited to 10 horsepower, making it one of the quietest of Algonquin's access lakes. Tom Thomson spent two summers working as a fire ranger on Grand Lake; this route goes by the windswept shores that gave him some of his most haunting visions. Until 1979 the tree that Thomson was painting when he produced the melancholy *Jack Pine* remained on the lakeshore. Thomson did the sketch for this painting from the small point on the left just before Grand Lake narrows and leads into the portage to Stratton Lake. He made the sketch in 1916, a year before his death, and even though the tree had been burned and was dead, it still stood until a storm toppled it in 1977. In 1979 canoe trippers used it to make a bonfire. Some experts believe that Thomson also painted *West Wind* on Grand

121

The Jack Pine, 1916–17 (Tom Thomson)

Lake, just to the right of the new ranger headquarters, where he had a summer cabin in 1915 and 1916. Others disagree, asserting that *West Wind* was painted on Cedar Lake.

The journey from Grand Lake southeast to St. Andrew's Lake is very easy. A 30-m portage south from Grand Lake over a long, low dam leads to Stratton Lake. This narrow, unruffled, dark green body of water is a joy to paddle. In late summer the afternoon sun shines on the campsites of the lake's eastern shore, inviting a lunchtime swim. At the south end of Stratton Lake is another short portage of 45 m around a small rapids which is not usually shootable.

St. Andrew's Lake, the only good-sized lake before the canyon, is rarely crowded. It is sensible to camp at this ideal spot and make the canyon a day trip, thus avoiding carrying one's gear all the way to the canyon and back. The last campsite on the left side of the lake is the loveliest because of its spaciousness and its sandy beach.

There are two possible routes from St. Andrew's to the Barron Canyon. The Barron River route includes four portages that add up to 2220 m; the Length Creek route has five portages totalling 4345 m. At first glance only a masochist would choose Length Creek, but it has the advantage of passing jewellike Cork Lake. The Barron River route's attraction is a big, booming falls right after St. Andrew's Lake. Neither of the two routes has difficult portages, and the paddling is minimal on both. Thus, for the sake of variety, this guide recommends travelling downstream to the Barron Canyon via the Barron River and back up to St. Andrew's lake via Length Creek.

Unlike the other five canoe trips described in this book, this trip is oriented towards a destination more spectacular than the journey. The canyon provides the only magnificent view included in the trip, and it is very much worth the travelling time.

After the Brigham Chute portage the route leads down the Barron Canyon beside cliffs that rise to breathtaking heights on either side of the river. The canyon was carved 10,000 years ago by a great wall of water that rushed through what is now Algonquin Park. Twelve thousand years ago the last of the four massive ice sheets that covered North America began to melt northward. In the melting, Lake Algonquin was born. It was a 129,500-square-kilometre meltwater lake that drowned the land from Chicago to Huntsville, but stopped short of present-day Algonquin Park. Five hundred years later the melting ice was pouring millions of litres of new water into the lake every day. The swelling waters of Lake Algonquin eventually broke their boundaries and created a new outlet just north of the future park. A torrent of water roared into Kioshkokwi Lake, carving a channel and flowing southeast to Cedar Lake and on to Radiant and Traverse lakes, then down two branches, the Petawawa and the Barron rivers. The wall of water, called by geologists the Fossmill Outlet, rushed through the Algonquin Park region for two or three centuries until Lake Algonquin had been entirely emptied.

All that remains of Lake Algonquin is Georgian Bay, but we have evidence of the Fossmill Outlet in the Barron Canyon. Besides the magnificently sculpted rock, the Outlet left behind small plants and tiny water creatures normally found much farther north. They remain as living relics of the glacial meltwater that created the canyon.

Today five important river systems originate in Algonquin Park: the Amable du Fond, the Muskoka, the Petawawa, the Bonnechere and the Madawaska, and they are all remnants of the great spillways that fed Lake Algonquin, which in turn fed the Champlain Sea to the east of it. The Barron River is a branch of the Petawawa River system, and as you paddle the Barron Canyon route, you are taking a journey along an ancient waterway that helped to shape Ontario.

Canoe Routes: Trip #4

The Nipissing River

The Nipissing, which snakes its way across the entire northeast corner of Algonquin Park, is not a big river like the Petawawa, with kilometres of rapids to set the adrenalin pumping, but it has subtle charms. Most of it is narrow; big pine trees guard its shores and wild snapdragons and lilac gentians bloom on its portages. Being one of Ontario's great trout rivers, in the springtime it attracts anglers who know every hole where trout rise to feed. This route is a ten-day trip, but one could shorten it to five days by going from North Tea Lake to High Falls and back.

In the 1920s, according to Ralph Bice, whose family used to trap in the park, big fragrant pines hung so far over both sides of the Nipissing River that their branches almost touched. None of these massive trees remains. The Nipissing was one of the park's great spring drive rivers; campers who follow this route will find remnants of old logging camps and river slides. It is also an interesting river to travel because of the variable terrain; you never know whether around the next bend you will encounter rock and pines or tall grass and marsh meadow.

The trip begins at Kawawaymog (Round) Lake. Although the lake is outside the park, it is necessary to buy an interior camping permit and a canoe routes map at the ranger station there. The drive from Toronto to Round Lake takes only an hour longer than the one from Toronto to Canoe Lake, and once on the route the area is rarely crowded. The map directions for finding the access point are sketchy. To reach the lake drive north from

Lilac and star and bird twined with the chant of my soul,
There in the fragrant pines and the cedars dusk and dim.
Walt Whitman (When Lilacs Last in the Dooryard Bloom'd)

Huntsville for one and three-quarters hours to South River. In South River turn right immediately north of the Texaco station and follow the road to the lake. There is at least one outfitter on Round Lake, where you can rent canoes and all other equipment.

The first two lakes, Round and North Tea, suffer the same maladies as all other access point lakes: they are crowded with noisy, often thoughtless campers who carry beer and radios. But a mere half-day's journey beyond North Tea Lake puts you in quiet back country.

It takes approximately two hours and two very easy portages to paddle from Round Lake to North Tea Lake. North Tea permits the use of small motorboats and has many beautiful campsites. The north shore of the lake, from opposite the westernmost large island to the big point (directly above the word "Tea" on the canoe routes map), was extensively logged during 1979 and 1980 approximately 100 m from the shoreline.

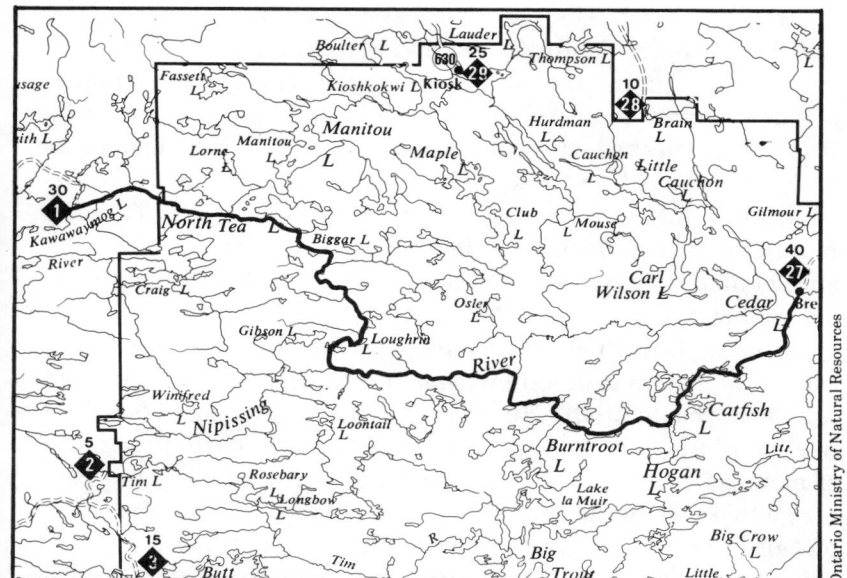

Canoe Trip #4

The route leaves North Tea via three short, easy portages and enters sparkling Biggar Lake. From Biggar onwards there will be few people on the river, except during the May trout season.

Now the route leads south from Biggar along Loughrin Creek, a narrow, winding stream that is rich with marsh wildlife. Both moose and great blue herons are common here. The 2010-m portage on Loughrin Creek is an easy walk, except for two steep hills, though in early spring it is muddy. After the portage it takes approximately one and a half hours to paddle Loughrin Creek, which twists and turns, seeming almost to wind back upon itself. You must lift your canoe over beaver dams, and if the water is low, you may have to use your paddle as a pole. This section can be frustrating to paddle in low water, but eventually it comes to an end.

Next come a series of very small lakes with short portages between them, all easy walks; even the final 1950-m-long portage before the Nipissing River is an easy trail.

This particular section of the Nipissing River is legendary for its speckled trout. They are most abundant in May when they rise from winter's depths to feed and to fill their air bladders, but even in late August they are easy to catch. The speckled trout is one of the most beautiful and delicious-tasting of all game fish. Its sides are flecked with ruby and gold, and in the frying pan its flesh turns sweet and juicy. These trout are not sold commercially; the only way to taste them is to catch them. There is nothing more delicious than the day's catch wrapped in foil with sliced onions, lemon juice and butter, and baked for twenty minutes in hot coals.

Until the late 1970s, when the government began restricting the use of motors to certain park lakes, hundreds of people would take motorboats up the Nipissing River every spring to fish. The new regulations have the double virtue of eliminating the noise of motors from the river and reducing the crowding, for few people go there when the only alternative is canoe travel. This factor has also probably prevented the river from being fished out.

Live bait fish are not permitted in Algonquin Park, for good reason. If unused minnows, such as perch, were dumped in lakes and rivers they would compete with trout for the available food and, being better hunters, would eventually take over. Live bait is not necessary for fishing on the Nipissing River, for the trout will take almost any lure that shines, though old Nipissing hands swear by Panther Martins. In the spring the best places to fish are pools just below rapids; in summer and fall look for trout where springs enter the river, cooling the water and adding oxygen to it.

There is an abandoned ranger cabin on the Nipissing River immediately west of Loughrin Creek (east of the portage to Gibson Lake) which has bunk beds for two people and one ancient spring bed, an old wood stove, a leaking roof and a large resident population of (harmless) garter snakes. For several generations, people who fish the Nipissing have been using High View Cabin as a refuge from torrential spring rains. The cabin survives through an informal network of travellers who cherish a place to get in out of the rain, and who maintain it by doing small repairs each time they use it or bring repair supplies whenever they pass through.

The first portage on the Nipissing River is an easy 345-m walk

Ontario Ministry of Natural Resources (APM 4406)

(a logging road crosses the river there). The river is approximately 20 m wide at this point, and the 25-m-high pine trees towering on the banks are grand reminders of the park's past. The next portage, a 2715-m trail around Allen Rapids, is another easy walk, followed by an extremely easy portage of 495 m around a rapids. There is a lovely campsite overlooking the falls here.

Several derelict cabins left over from logging camps appear on the next portage, which is an easy 365-m trail. The stretch of water from this portage to High Falls offers the best fishing on the river; pool after pool yield feisty 900-g speckled trout.

The next landmark is the spectacular High Falls: two large

roaring waterfalls, which have splendid pools for swimming. High Falls is on an 1190-m portage which is not difficult except for one steep hill at the outset. The most pleasurable campsite in this area is below the falls, beside the small murmuring rapids.

After High Falls the fishing deteriorates, and the route leaves the river via the 1930-m portage into Ramona Lake. This portage is a gentle but relentless uphill walk all the way, its only saving grace a canoe rest halfway along. One hundred metres before the end of the portage a gravel road crosses the trail; to find the portage trail after the road, make a jog to the right.

The route continues towards Burntroot Lake by means of small portages and short paddles; the lovely small lakes Whiskeyjack and Robinson are both a sparkling emerald green, and the superb island campsite on Robinson Lake has an especially fine view.

The 1285-m portage into the north end of Burntroot Lake is easy. Along the lake's north shore, from near the end of the portage trail as far east as Perley Lake, a great deal of logging took place in 1978 and 1979, an area that had been logged many times before. Mr. Perley, for whom the lake was named, was one of the first loggers in Algonquin Park; he owned the timber rights to most of the territory along this canoe route. The Algonquin Forestry Authority, which carries out all logging in the park, wants to build a permanent year-round road over the Nipissing River northeast of Perley Lake so it can haul logs through the park to market instead of having to go the longer distances around the park's perimeter. As of this writing, permission for this road has not yet been granted.

The route leaves tranquil Perley Lake via the Petawawa River, and in quick succession there are four small, easy portages into magnificent Catfish Lake. The first large island on Catfish Lake has one of the most beautiful campsites in Algonquin Park. It is reached by a climb up from the water; once there campers have a hawk's view of the lake. The many tent spots are carpeted by pine needles, and below there is a large expanse of flat rock beach.

Four portages lead eastward out of Catfish Lake: the first is only 80 m long; the second is 170 m; the third is a long 2345 m; the fourth is 255 m and has a glorious 7-m falls at the end. All four of these trails are easy, especially the last two, which slope gently downhill. From there to Cedar Lake extensive logging has been carried out in the past five years.

After a short paddle the route leads to a 715-m portage into Cedar Lake, an easy walk down a gradual hill. A path to the left approximately 150 m along this trail takes you to a spectacular 9-m waterfall with the remains of an old logging chute at its top, and a sharp, boulder-rimmed drop. This interesting sight is worth the side trip.

Cedar Lake is majestic. Some experts believe that Tom Thomson painted *West Wind* here, and their assertion is plausible, for the far windswept shores of the lake convey the spirit of the rugged Canadian wilderness. Boats of unlimited horsepower and waterskiing are both permitted on Cedar Lake, but few people bring their boats such as a distance from the city, and the few craft that do appear are dwarfed by the lake's grandeur.

The trip ends with a long paddle across Cedar Lake to the ghost town of Brent, which was a thriving lumber town at the turn of the century. The Canadian Northern Railway was completed in 1915 and had a station at Brent. It brought Kish-Kaduk Lodge to the lake but, like the other railway hotels, Kish-Kaduk is now gone. The Brent lumber mill closed in 1931, and little remains of the town's prosperous past. A few former residents of the town now make their summer homes there, and the Canadian National Railways still maintains a station including a shiny new bunkhouse for its crews.

Campers who have paddled to Brent before will remember the proprietor of the general store, Smiling Gerry, so named for his dour countenance. An accountant with the Gillis Lumber Company, he left their employ in 1936 to open the store. It was a Brent ritual among canoe trippers to celebrate the end of a week in the bush with a cold coke from Gerry's cooler. Gerry could be utterly unfriendly, even downright mean, to the campers who swarmed through his store like locusts. But what few people knew is that anyone who arrived in Brent sick or rain-drenched could always count on him for help. He would take them in, feed them, and make up beds for them for the night. Gerry died of a stroke in January 1981, and his store was bought by Algonquin Outfitters, who now run a businesslike outfitting depot. Gerry's passing marks the end of an era in Algonquin Park.

Joanne Kates

Come, flaunt the brief prerogative of life,
Dip your small civilized foot in this cold water
And ripple, for a moment, the smooth surface of time.

F. R. Scott (Surfaces)

Canoe Routes: Trip #5

Opeongo–Laveille Circuit

This trip encompasses the big lakes at the heart of Algonquin Park —the grand, windy and wild bodies of water. Sometimes the winds blow up so fiercely on these lakes that canoeists must take refuge on shore and spend the afternoon watching the whitecaps dance. At other times the water can be as still as shining glass. This route is never crowded; most people are put off by a 5305-m portage, which except for its length is not difficult, particularly since it is reached on the last day of the trip, when food packs have been lightened. Trip #5 normally takes five days, though you can shorten it into a weekend excursion by taking the water taxi up Opeongo Lake and paddling to Big Crow Lake; this version will still give you time for a day trip to a stand of virgin pines—one of the trip's highlights. Especially in spring, fishing is superb on this circuit; there are lake trout and smallmouth bass in the lakes and speckled trout in the river.

The trip begins at the Opeongo Lake access point, which is easy to find from Highway 60. Opeongo is the park's largest lake and is not suitable for novice paddlers except on its rare glassy days; it can blow up into metre-high waves that can swamp a canoe. Opeongo Outfitters will take campers and canoes up the lake to the portage into Proulx Lake for about $25 per canoe. Reservations must be made in advance, by telephone (705-637-5470) or by mail (Box 123, Whitney, Ontario K0J 2M0). They also provide a complete canoe trip outfitting service.

If the lake is not too windy it takes about a day to paddle from

133

the access point to the Proulx Lake portage. Opeongo—an Algonquin Indian name meaning "place where there are beaches of sand"—is majestic, so big that even the motorboats of unlimited horsepower do not disturb it. And fortunately for canoeists there are few of them.

The 1390-m portage into Proulx Lake is an easy walk on a flat trail, the last part being as wide as a road. After Proulx Lake comes a lovely creek paddle, and then the route goes through Little Crow Lake into Big Crow Lake. The regulation permitting motors of up to six horsepower on both these lakes except in July and August enables anglers to fish them in motorboats during the spring fishing season. Fishing campers drive their boats to the Proulx Lake portage, wheel them to the end of the portage on homemade two-wheel dollies, hide the dollies in the woods, and motor to Big Crow Lake for the fishing.

Big Crow is so sandy and its drop so gradual that it is possible to walk great distances out into the lake from the beaches. One of its finest campsites is the last one on the left. The route goes due east through the lake. At its south end a ranger tower can be reached by climbing the trail from the cabin on the shore. The tower is more than 30 m tall and sits on a 100-m cliff; the view is worth the climb.

After the route leaves Big Crow Lake it goes along the Crow River for approximately half a day. This section is very beautiful. The river ranges from 25 m to 75 m in width, has large pine trees and cedars sheltering its banks, and contains many springs where speckled trout congregate during the summer. It is also a river with a history. There are old logging dams and side piers, relics of the period when logs were driven down the river to market every spring.

The first portage is an easy 240-m trail. Approximately halfway along it are the remains of an old log drive camp on the left. A stand of virgin pine trees can be reached from this portage on a path that leads to the right just after its beginning. This side trail first crosses the river on an old logging dam, which still has the ramshackle remnants of the large spillway that was used for shooting logs downriver. The walk to and from the virgin pines takes just over an hour and a half and goes through woods where painted trilliums bloom in spring and where the sun filters

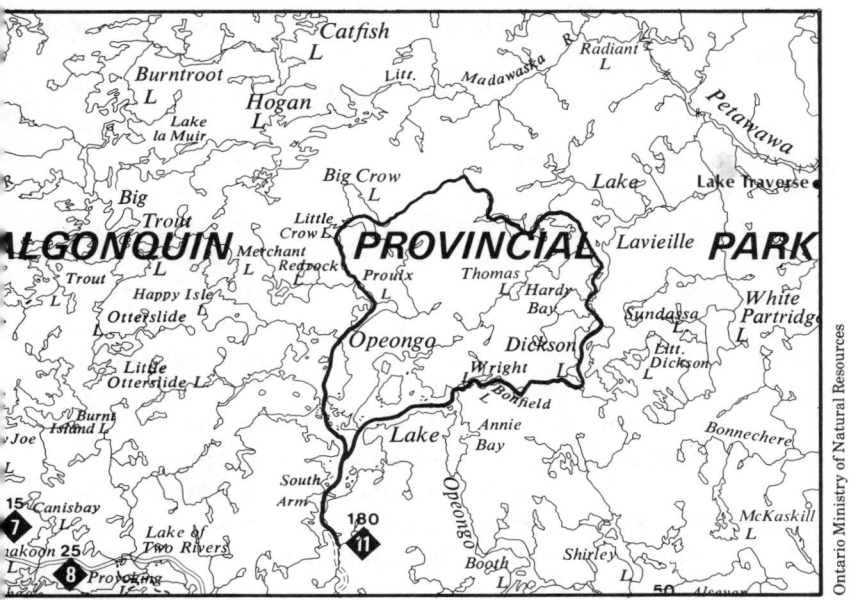

Ontario Ministry of Natural Resources

Canoe Trip #5

through the treetops in radiant columns. The 300-year-old pines are a natural sight one encounters all too rarely; their broad trunks are immense and their tops tower above the hardwood canopy.

Those white pine trees were officially protected from logging in 1939 by Frank MacDougall, superintendent of Algonquin Park from 1939 to 1941. MacDougall had an important influence on the park. He bought its first airplane, an open cockpit biplane, and learned to fly it. Since then many crews have saved thousands of hectares of park forest from destruction by detecting and fighting fires from the air.

MacDougall was also a fierce and effective protector of the park's flora. As one of the first people to see the conflict between logging and natural growth, he established regulations to protect the Crow River white pines, and he also set up the park's first shoreline reserves to limit the effects of logging. When Mac-Dougall died, the section of Highway 60 that runs through Algonquin Park was renamed the Frank MacDougall Parkway.

After the excursion to the virgin pines the route continues

along the Crow River, which has narrowed and now twists and turns through a gentle landscape. Camping on this part of the river is not advisable because of the many insects, but the fishing for speckled trout is excellent. The water level on the Crow is usually too low for shooting any of the rapids and there are numerous rocks under the surface, so the person in the bow of the canoe should be especially watchful. The river portages are all easy trails.

The Algonquin Forestry Authority is fighting to build a permanent, year-round road over the Crow River near the 1220-m portage. As of this writing, the government has not yet allowed the building of this road.

As the route nears Crow Bay the river widens. The first campsite to the right of the bay is on a picturesque long point; the site is windy enough to be free of bugs and is blessed with east and west exposures giving campers a view of both sunrise and sunset.

The route leaves Crow Bay via a wide channel that opens into Lake Laveille, another beautiful body of water. In 1615 Samuel de Champlain's geographer gave it his name. Laveille is almost as big as Opeongo Lake, and the wind can blow up on it just as fiercely. It is not unusual for Lake Laveille to be crowned with 60-cm-high waves, and at these times canoeing on it resembles a roller coaster ride.

Lake Laveille is on the spring fishing circuit, so motorboats of up to six horsepower are permitted there except for July and August. The north end of Hardy Bay is the favoured fishing spot for lake trout. Laveille has many fine campsites. The first one on the left after the channel from Crow Bay is particularly lovely; it is large and offers a panoramic view of the lake.

From Hardy Bay into Dickson Lake there is a 90-m portage. Dickson is a windblown lake the colour of jade, lined on its eastern shore with red pines that are nearly 350 years old. Like Laveille, it is a spring trout fishing lake and has the same motorboat regulations.

Dickson Lake was named for one of the two men who were responsible for the creation of Algonquin Park. James Dickson was sent by the government to survey the area for settlement and farming during the 1880s. He was one of the first people to argue that the land was extremely unpromising for agriculture because of its thin, sour soil and short growing season. He also thought the area would be a glorious vacation land, and in his journal expressed surprise that "so few tourists and seekers after romantic scenery visit the head waters of the Muskoka [Oxtongue], Petawawa and Madawaska rivers . . . and the lakes are unrivalled for scenery." In Dickson's view, another reason to create a park was to put some limitations on logging; he was distressed that the area south of the Tim River had been "cut in a very careless and extravagant manner." Dickson joined with his colleague Alexander Kirkwood to lobby for the creation of Algonquin Park and in 1893 they were successful.

The route leaves Dickson Lake via a 5303-m portage. For such a long portage this is far more benign than one would expect. The trail is relatively flat and contains few catwalks; if canoe campers rest for five minutes at twenty-minute intervals, they can make the portage in two hours.

Approximately 1200 m along the trail there is a fork; the right branch leads uphill to an old logging road which goes all the way south to the East Arm of Opeongo Lake. Anglers put their boats on two-wheel dollies and use this trail because the regular trail, though shorter, is narrow and bumpy.

The left fork—the regular portage—leads to Bonfield Lake. At the fork there are the tumbledown remains of an old logging camp. Just before the end of this trail there is a long—almost 100 m—series of easy catwalks lashed together.

Then there are two short portages separated by a small lake, after which the route leads into the East Arm of Opeongo Lake. If the wind is not high it will take no more than two hours to paddle down the East Arm to the narrows at its southern end. Just before that narrows a clearing on the left shore reveals all that remains of Sunnyside, which was Capt. John Dennison's farm. Dennison was a legendary park settler who wrestled a bear and lost. Near the shore a rock cairn with a copper plaque reading "At Rest" marks Captain John's grave.

Dennison was an English military man who came to Canada to farm. But the steady life of a farmer did not suit the swashbuckling old soldier; in 1870, aged 71, he and his two sons with their wives and children moved to Sunnyside on Lake Opeongo. They were not the first people to discover the beauty of the area. Until they were forced north in the middle of the eighteenth century, Algonquin Indians used to camp at the lake every summer. The remnants of that tribe now live on a reservation near Killaloe.

Captain John and his family cleared 240 hectares of the wilderness at Sunnyside and there they grew food for their own sustenance and to sell to logging camps around the lake. In addition to farming they earned money by trapping. One day in 1881 Dennison paddled up to the North Arm of Opeongo Lake with his eight-year-old grandson to check his trapline. He had set a bear trap there the week before, at the portage into Happy Isle Lake. As he stuck his head over the large fallen log in front of the trap an enormous bear, mad with pain from the steel clamp of the trap, clawed at Captain John and dragged him over the log. The captain screamed to his grandson to go for help.

The boy paddled the 15 km back to Sunnyside; but his father was on a hunting trip and it was a few days before they returned to the trap. There they found evidence of a terrible struggle. Captain John's clothes, everything save his boots, had been torn to shreds. He was dead and, according to park legend, so was the bear. The boy and his father took the body back to Sunnyside and buried it there. The Dennison family was disheartened by the captain's death, and in 1885 they left Sunnyside. It subsequently became a lumber camp depot farm, supplying fresh vegetables to logging camps in the summers.

After Sunnyside the route goes through the short narrows into the main part of Opeongo Lake, and then down the lake; on a calm day this will take approximately two hours. It is also possible to arrange in advance to be picked up by the Opeongo Outfitters' water taxi at the north end of the East Arm.

At the turn of the century J.R. Booth built a railroad spur line to take timber from the Opeongo area out of the park. He owned the timber limits in most of the area of this route, and a great deal more timber as well; his company was at that time one of the largest lumber companies in the world.

J.R. Booth was born in 1827, the son of a poor Quebec homesteader. In 1852 he left Quebec and came to Ottawa as a carpenter with his wife and child; he had $9 in his pocket. Soon Booth owned a small logging business. In 1857 Ottawa was chosen to be the capital of Canada, and Booth, through clever under-bidding, got the contract to supply the wood for the new parliament buildings. Except for the parliamentary library, which still stands, the buildings are gone, burned to the ground in 1916. Booth made a $15,000 profit on the contract, and with that capital he built an empire.

In 1897 he bought the Egan Estate timber limits, which comprised 388 square kilometres of prime pine trees. Most of that land is now in Algonquin Park. The profits he made on the timber are the stuff of which entrepreneurial legends are made. By 1894 J.R. Booth owned timber licences to more than 10,000 square kilometres of land, and 1500 men were working for him. He was a millionaire many times over, thanks in part to the giant pine trees that stood on this canoe route.

Business was good, but J.R. thought there must be a more efficient way than river drives to get the logs out of the park. He built a railway line from Parry Sound to Ottawa, crossing through the park on the way. Booth used the trains to carry logs from his Algonquin Park limits to the mills of Ottawa, and to carry western grain to eastern markets. For a time his line was the busiest one in Canada, and a by-product was the opening of the park to tourism. Grand Trunk Railway took over J.R. Booth's rail line in 1905 and then sold it to Canadian National Railways in 1918. In 1959 Canadian National abandoned it and the age of rail transport in the park was over.

Joanne Kates

Suffused with sun, the forest glows.
The sunbeams rise in pillared dust.

. . . .

The forest's absolutely hushed,
As though the life of that deep dell
Were by the gleaming sun not ambushed,
But mastered by another spell.

Boris Pasternak (Silence)

Canoe Route: Trip #6

The Petawawa River (Cedar Lake to McManus Lake)

The difference between river travel and lake travel could be described in literary terms as the difference between reading a novel and a short story. Canoeing down the Petawawa River is like reading a novel; you find yourself involved with various characters along the route—the railway tracks that follow the river, the riverside vegetation, the rapids, the current, the rocks on the shore. And as these characters reappear and change, they are greeted like old friends with whom you have developed an ongoing relationship.

This complete trip, from Cedar Lake to the park's eastern boundary at McManus Lake, takes ten days, including a one-day side trip to Eustache Lake. But the trip is easily shortened: dedicated river runners who want to avoid portages begin their trip at the Lake Traverse access point and spend four or five exciting days running the rapids down the river to McManus Lake. What these people miss, however, is the isolation and the tranquillity of the lush country from Cedar Lake to Lake Traverse. From Traverse onward the river is crowded.

The Petawawa's headwaters rise in the rocky highlands at the centre of the park. Gathering in the Tim River, the Nipissing and the Crow, it speeds along to Cedar Lake. Between Cedar and McManus lakes the river narrows in many places and the current quickens into foaming, boiling rapids. After McManus it widens and flows more gently to the Ottawa River, where it mingles its waters with those flowing to the St. Lawrence and the sea.

The Indians who first inhabited the shores of the river named it after its many rapids: Petawawa, "a noise is heard far away." The first whites to see the river were members of a British exploring party, led by Alexander Shirreff in 1829, who were looking for suitable farmland on which to settle. Shirreff caught an 18-kg lake trout in Cedar Lake, which endeared the area to him. Then came the shantymen, the loggers who camped below each set of rapids in order to shepherd the logs downriver in spring. The last river drive on the Petawawa took place in 1945.

The Petawawa River has claimed many lives, and a canoe trip on it should not be taken lightly. *It is suitable only for expert canoeists possessing white water skills.* The Petawawa is one of the best white water rivers in southern Ontario, and people having the skills will fall in love with it, especially with Rollway and Schooner rapids. But the relationships are all on its terms. On the first half of the trip, from Cedar Lake to Lake Traverse, it is necessary to portage around most of the rapids, but from Lake Traverse onwards many of the rapids can be shot.

It is important for novice white water paddlers to realize that running white water is not a skill that can be self-taught, and the Petawawa River is not a good place to begin learning it. A beginner should start on smaller rivers with an instructor present. Furthermore, every section of every rapids *must* be scouted by the paddler before deciding to shoot it. The fact that one person shoots a particular set of rapids in a particular canoe does not mean that someone else can also do it. Nor does the fact that this book suggests a rapids is shootable mean that anyone can shoot it. Depending on their shape and construction, canoes vary enormously in their seaworthiness in fast water. The water level on the river changes from year to year and from month to month. And of course one's skill level also determines which rapids one can shoot. A useful guideline when deciding whether to shoot rapids is that if you cannot "read" the water and thereby make a prior decision exactly how to handle each part of the rapids, you cannot shoot it safely. The Petawawa is a big river and it gives few second chances.

You begin this trip at the Cedar Lake (Brent) access point, leaving the highway and driving to Cedar Lake via the Wendigo Lake access point. (The wendigo is a mythical creature who

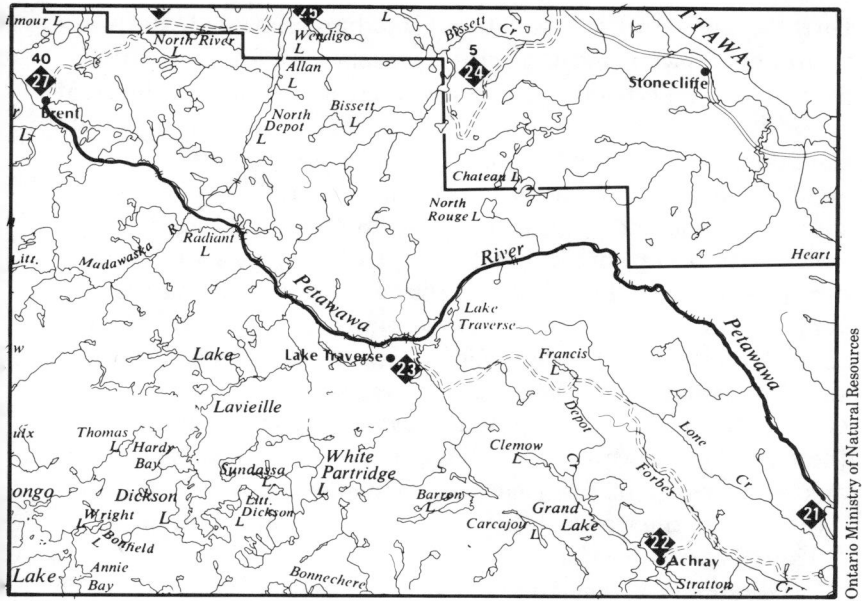

Ontario Ministry of Natural Resources

Canoe Trip #6

appears, it is said, in the form of a green mist or sometimes as a human with hair covering its face, arms and legs. The Algonquin Indians believed that the wendigo was once a human but that it had been driven by hunger to eat human flesh and was punished by being turned into a monster.)

Cedar Lake is a big, beautiful and often windy body of water. The route leaves the lake via a 960-m portage which leads into the Petawawa River. This set of rapids is not shootable, but the portage is fairly easy, except for one bad hill to climb. The short paddle to the next portage is a fine introduction to the river as it winds between big pines on a rocky shore.

The 685-m portage is also around rapids that are not shootable. Looking downriver from the beginning of the portage, you may be tempted to put your canoe in the water, but the rapids around the bend are far more dangerous than those in the first section. This change bears out the primary rule of white water travel: before you shoot, scout every part.

Just before the 860-m portage around Devil's Chute there is a large railway trestle bridge; and 100 m before the end of that portage, the trail crosses the Canadian National Railways main line. This portage is tolerable, except for a few steep hills.

Next there is a long and glorious river paddle into Radiant Lake. The shore slopes so gradually here that you can walk into the lake for more than a kilometre before the water is over your head. There are four spectacular campsites on the north shore of the lake immediately east of the North River, and each has its own sandy beach, birch forests and driftwood logs which make hot fires. Radiant Lake has six cottages on it and small motorboats are permitted, but it is essentially a quiet lake and few canoe trippers pass through. Only the distant rumble of the railway trains disturbs its peacefulness. However, the western shore of the lake is less attractive than the north shore. Near Odenback there is a logging camp whose diesel generator pierces the silence at certain times of the year; and Canadian National Railways owns land on the western shore where it maintains buildings.

There is evidence that people have been camping on the shores of Radiant Lake for 5000 years. Archaeologists have found ground slate hunting tools and pottery fragments there, which indicate the presence of Indians of the Archaic Period.

It takes approximately three days to paddle from Radiant Lake to Lake Traverse. A year-round logging road crosses the river shortly after Radiant, and just past the lake is Squirrel Rapids with a 230-m portage around it. Given the right conditions, this rapids is shootable.

The Petawawa is an excellent river for catching smallmouth bass, and below Squirrel Rapids there are pools where bass abound. Daredevil lures work well here, especially at dusk when the fish are rising to feed.

The route continues downriver to a 695-m portage which skirts Big Sawyer Rapids and Battery Rapids. A logging road crosses the portage. On this section of the river, and farther downstream as well, you will see giant pine logs and large stumps, a legacy of the spring drives of the past. Some of the stumps are left from trees that were cut for timber; others are there because thousands of trees died along the shorelines when logging companies built dams to hold back the water in preparation for the drives.

Neither Big Sawyer not Battery Rapids is shootable, but the portage is not difficult. There are no hills or catwalks; the railway tracks across the trail signal the end of the portage. In early summer look for wild irises growing along this pretty path.

After Battery Rapids the river winds through soft marshy country, with purple pickerelweed growing in the shallows and long grasses waving in the breeze. Then there are two 70-m portages around white water that can be shot under the right conditions.

After a very short paddle the route comes to Cascade Rapids—which is not shootable—and the 500-m portage around it. Although the trail is not hilly, it is rendered difficult by fallen trees, especially at its beginning. In August cardinal flowers bloom in scarlet splendour at this point on the riverbank.

The next portage is an easy 180 m over the railroad track into Francis Lake. Under the right conditions this rapids can be shot. The railway line follows the river closely here, and six times a day long trains roll by.

The route leaves Francis Lake via two small portages of 140 m and 155 m past unshootable rapids. Next there is a long, lovely paddle down to a 390-m portage around an unshootable rapids, and then another fine paddle to another set of unshootable rapids skirted by a 1400-m portage. This trail is poorly marked, but the terrain is not difficult. By now the pine and spruce are giving way to hardwood forest of oak and birch and majestic maples.

The river narrows here, and there are two short portages of 200 m and 275 m. At this point the portages become somewhat rougher; rocks on the trails make the footing more difficult. The first of these two short portages has an obscure trail; to follow it, look for blazes on trees and small cairns.

If you can afford the time, it is worthwhile to make camp on the beautiful river campsite just above the 200-m portage and then make a day trip to Eustache Lake for lunch, carrying only a lunch pack. Eustache Lake, the deepest lake in Algonquin Park, is reached via a 2650-m portage from the Petawawa. Cliffs 25 m high ring the lake and continue below the water for another 90 m; on a clear day you can see far into the lake's depths. The lake was carved out of Precambrian granite by the Fossmill Outlet that drained Lake Algonquin after the last ice age receded 11,000 years ago, and there are still tiny Arctic crustaceans in it from that period.

The hike to Eustache Lake begins on the railway tracks, which abound with wild strawberries in July and blackberries and raspberries in July and August. Past the tracks the trail continues through a lovely hardwood forest dotted with pine trees. The easy trail is little used but not hard to follow. There are trout in the lake and wild roses and lavender asters on the shore. Follow the trail partway around the lake to the second campsite on the peninsula for the most attractive lunch spot; this site overlooks the spectacular lakeside cliffs.

Back on the main Petawawa River route, there is a short paddle down to two portages (550 m and 1050 m) past rapids that cannot be shot. Immediately after the 1050-m portage there is a turn in the river and suddenly on the right a monstrous white disc protrudes above the trees. This is the Lake Traverse radio telescope, part of a federal government National Research Council settlement on the lakeshore. Approximately thirty people live here doing research in the field of astronomy. There is a small hotel for visiting scientists as well as several houses, an apartment house, and other buildings. The facility resembles an urban subdivision, and conservationists have charged that it has no place in a provincial park.

The route enters Lake Traverse via an easy, almost flat 660-m portage. The end of the portage is also the Lake Traverse access point, where many river runners begin their four- or five-day trip. At the south end of Lake Traverse, on both sides of the gravel road that runs from Achray to the Traverse access point, clear-cut logging took place until 1977. This area has since been replanted.

After Lake Traverse the river winds between tall evergreen-strewn cliffs and narrowing gorges. There is a long, glorious paddle and then a 345-m portage around Big Thompson Rapids, which is not shootable. The portage is easy with one exception: a very short hill so steep that it is impossible for one person carrying a canoe or a pack to climb it without help. From here to Crooked Chute there was a great deal of logging on the south side of the river from 1975 until 1981. If you walk 100 m back from the shoreline, the logged areas will be visible.

The route leads to Little Thompson Rapids, which is not shootable; the 165-m portage around the rapids is not difficult. Next

The Natch

comes a beautiful paddle to Grillade Rapids—shootable under the right conditions—or its 130-m portage, and then a 425-m portage around another rapids that is also shootable under the right conditions.

Campsites are few and far between from Grillade Rapids to McManus Lake, and so many river runners begin the trip at Lake Traverse that it is wise to camp early.

Crooked Chute is the river's first piece of big white water that can be shot under the right conditions. But caution is necessary. Note the grave with a cross for the river driver who did not leave Crooked Chute alive. It is possible—after scouting—to stay on the river and shoot the beginning of Crooked Chute until the point where the river makes a sharp left turn and then a very sharp, almost 90-degree, turn to the right. You will not be able to see around the bend of the river after the right turn, and your natural tendency is to swing out and take the turn on the left side of the river. DON'T. Keep to the right and watch for a campsite marker, which is easily seen, on the right shore. Paddle hard across the current and land at the campsite. If you look 100 m downstream just before landing, the reason for not continuing will be obvious: the river compresses to about half its previous width, and the water begins to boil. There is a 5-m "staircase" and, at the bottom of an old log chute, a turn so crooked that a canoe would surely dump. After landing at the campsite on the right, campers will walk the last 600 m of the 1580-m Crooked Chute portage. The trail here is not difficult but finding it can be confusing. Look for the path that goes through the woods, not alongside the river.

Again the river becomes quiet and there is a short paddle down to an easy 120-m portage. Then there is another short paddle to Rollway Rapids, one of southern Ontario's famous rapids and also one of its most dangerous. Only advanced white water canoeists should consider shooting it. A memorial plaque at Rollway commemorates the death of journalist Blair Fraser, who died shooting this rapids. Fraser was an expert white water canoeist who was on a spring trip with other experienced rapids runners. He and his partner missed the place where they intended to land and shot Rollway Rapids by accident. The canoe took in water and sank in the first few standing waves; Blair Fraser drowned even though he was wearing a life preserver. In May in Algonquin Park the water is still so cold that a person cannot live in it long enough to swim to shore, even when wearing a life jacket. The portage around Rollway Rapids is an easy 820 m.

Now the route leads to the river's most magnificent section. Cliffs begin to rise and flowers bloom in colourful array: wild irises and roses on the lakeshores, fuschia anemones on the portages, crimson cardinal flowers on the riverbanks, purple pickerelweed and tall white yarrow in the marshes.

Getting to The Natch (designated on your canoe routes map) is somewhat confusing. The map indicates only a 275-m portage, but in reality this portage is in two parts separated by a short paddle. The first part is around a rapids that is not shootable, and the path is very poor—hard to find and difficult to walk. Then comes a short paddle and another portage sign, which is not indicated on the map. This section is shootable under the right conditions. Shortly afterwards there is a campsite on the north shore of the river. Plan to arrive at this site early in the day, not only because competition for campsites is keen on this part of the Petawawa but also because the campsite is possessed of spectacular beauty. It sits under the magnificent 100-m cliffs of The Natch with their rare, smooth cliff-brake ferns. Long ago The Natch was a holy Indian gathering place; there were Indian petroglyphs of animals on the cliff face and Indian huts on the shores. In fall Indians congregated here to feast in celebration of nature's summer bounty. Both petroglyphs and huts are gone, but the enchantment of the area remains.

After The Natch the river becomes a playground for lovers of white water. Two portages of 135 m and 160 m skirt rapids that cannot be shot, but beyond this point most of the rapids can be shot under the right conditions. Schooner Rapids is as famous as Rollway for its challenges. The portage around it is 2305 m. After Schooner the route crosses a major hydro transmission line, and then there is a 1400-m portage around another set of rapids that can be shot under the right conditions. By now the water is moving so fast that the shore seems to be flying by, and you sense that your time on the river is almost over.

The route leads next to a 3400-m portage around Fivemile Rapids, which is shootable under the right conditions. After

Fivemile the landscape softens around the edges and begins to take on the characteristics of a southern forest; silver maples appear and evergreens give way to basswood and sumac and ash.

The route leads through Whitson Lake, which is only a temporary widening of the river, and the river narrows again. There is a 500-m portage around fast water which is shootable under the right conditions. Then the route leads through Smith Lake, another temporary widening of the river, after which there is a 90-m portage around a rapids, also shootable under the right conditions.

This rapids leads into McManus Lake, which though pleasant is polluted by the debris and noise common to all access points.

After living on the great Petawawa River for five to ten days, after drinking it, swimming in it, catching smallmouth bass in it, being tossed by its foaming white water and carried by its current, there is no happy way to take your leave.

Terry Sullivan

APPENDIXES

Park Facilities

Information Services—Information and brochures
West Gate, km 0 (April—Thanksgiving)
East Gate, km 55.8 (April—Thanksgiving)
Cache Lake, km 23.3 (April—Labour Day)
   Or write to: Ministry of Natural Resources,
   Box 219, Whitney, Ont.   K0J 2M0

Picnic Grounds

Canisbay Lake
Costello Creek (no beach)
Hardwood Hill
Lake of Two Rivers
Little Madawaska
Oxtongue River (no beach)
Tea Lake Dam

Campgrounds

   Chlorinated water; vault toilets (except as noted)
   No electrical hook-ups
Canisbay Lake (242 sites)
Coon Lake (48 sites)
Kearney (104 sites)—flush toilets, hot water
Mew Lake (155 sites)—flush toilets, showers,
   laundry facilities
Opeongo (23 sites)
Pog Lake (281 sites)—flush toilets, showers,
   laundry facilities; priority given to reservations
Rock Lake (126 sites)
Tea Lake (54 sites)
Two Rivers (241 sites)
Whitefish Lake (19 sites)—youth groups,
   reservations only

Interpretive Program

Park Museum (open weekends in spring; daily in summer and fall)
Pioneer Logging Exhibit (open weekends in spring and fall; daily in
   summer)
Pog Lake Theatre (evening programs, daily in summer)

Conducted Hikes (daily in summer)

Stores

Two Rivers Store (km 31.4)
Portage Store (km 14.1)—includes restaurant, gas
  pumps, and canoe trip outfitting

Private Lodges

Arowhon Pines Lodge (km 15.4) 705-633-5661 or 416-483-4393
Bartlett Lodge (km 23.3) 705-633-5543
Killarney Lodge (km 33.2) 705-633-5551, or 800-461-1117

Guides and Organizations

Canoe-Trip Outfitters and/or Guides

Algonquin Canoe Routes Limited, Whitney, Ont. K0J 2M0 (705) 637-
  2699

Cedar Routes, P.O. Box 191, Sta. R, Toronto, Ont. M4G 3Z9 (416) 961-
  6792

Madawaska Kanu Camp Inc., P.O. Box 365, Barry's Bay, Ont. K0J 1B0;
  Winter: 2 Tuna Court, Don Mills, Ont. M3A 3L1 (416) 447-8845

Northern Wilderness Outfitters, Box 89, South River, Ont. P0A 1X0
  (705) 474-3272; Winter: R.R. #9, Brampton, Ont. L6T 3Z8

Portage and Opeongo Stores, Algonquin Park, Ont. P0A 1B0 (705) 633-
  5622

Travel Cuts' Canadian Wilderness Trips, 44 St. George St., Toronto,
  Ont. K5S 2E4 (416) 979-2604

Cross-Country Ski Touring

Algonquin Nordic Ski Touring, 40 Dixington Cres., Suite 404, Weston,
  Ont. M9P 2K8 (416) 248-6325

Conservation Organizations

Algonquin Wildlands League, Suite 308, 47 Colborne St., Toronto, Ont.
  M5E 1E3

Canadian Environmental Law Association, 1 Spadina Cres., Suite 303,
  Toronto, Ont. M5S 2J5

Federation of Ontario Naturalists, 355 Lesmill Road, Don Mills, Ont.
  M5V 2B1

Pollution Probe, University of Toronto, 43 Queen's Park Cres., Toronto,
  Ont. M5S 1A1

Sierra Club of Ontario, 47 Colborne St., Toronto, Ont., M5E 1E3

REFERENCES

Ontario Ministry of Natural Resources: Algonquin Park Publications*

Books

A Pictorial History of Algonquin Provincial Park (1980)
Birds of Algonquin Provincial Park (1980)
Fishing in Algonquin Provincial Park (1980)
Mammals of Algonquin Provincial Park (1978)
Reptiles and Amphibians of Algonquin Park (1976)
Wildflowers of Algonquin Provincial Park (1980)

Nature Trail Guides

Beaver Pond Trail (Algonquin Beaver Ecology)
Booth's Rock Trail (Man and the Algonquin Environment)
Hardwood Lookout Trail (Algonquin Hardwood Forest Ecology)
Hemlock Bluff Trail (Research in Algonquin)
Lookout Trail (Algonquin Geology)
Peck Lake Trail (Ecology of an Algonquin Lake)
Two Rivers Trail (Changes in the Algonquin Forests)
Spruce Bog Boardwalk (Algonquin Spruce Bog Ecology)
Whiskey Rapids Trail (Algonquin River Ecology)

Maps

Algonquin Provincial Park Hiking Trails for Back Packers
Algonquin Provincial Park Canoe Routes, 1982

* These publications are available for a nominal fee at the Park Museum, the Information Centre, and the District Office (East Gate); or by writing to Ministry of Natural Resources, Box 219, Whitney, Ont. K0J 2M0.

Further Reading

Addison, Ottelyn. *Early Days in Algonquin Park.* Toronto: McGraw-Hill Ryerson, 1974.

———, with Harwood, Elizabeth. *Tom Thomson: The Algonquin Years.* Toronto: Ryerson Press, 1969.

Algonquin Wildlands League. *Wilderness Now.* Toronto: New Press, 1971.

American National Red Cross. *Canoeing.* New York: Doubleday & Co., 1977.

Berglund, Berndt. *The Complete Wilderness Almanac.* Toronto: Pagurian Press, 1977.

Bice, Ralph. *Along the Trail with Ralph Bice.* Toronto: Consolidated Amethyst Communications, 1980.

Brunnelle, Hasse. *The Back-Packer's Food Book.* New York: Simon & Schuster, 1981.

Davidson, James West, and Rugge, John. *The Complete Wilderness Paddler.* New York: Alfred A. Knopf, 1976.

Drew, Edwin P. *The Complete Light-Pack Camping and Trail-Foods Cookbook.* New York: McGraw-Hill, 1977.

Franks, C.E.S. *The Canoe and White Water.* Toronto: University of Toronto Press, 1977.

Freeman, Bill. *Shantymen of Cache Lake.* Toronto: James Lorimer & Co., 1975.

Guillet, G.R. *Algonquin Provincial Park, a geological guide to Highway 60.* Toronto: Ontario Dept. of Mines and Northern Affairs, 1969.

Hodgins, Carol. *Wanapitei, Canoe-Trippers' Cookbook.* Cobalt, Ont.: Highway Bookshop, 1982.

Jacobson, Cliff. *Wilderness Canoeing and Camping.* New York: E.P. Dutton, 1977.

Kinmount, Vikki and Axcell, Claudia. *Simple Foods for the Pack.* San Francisco: Sierra Club Books, 1976.

Little, William T. *The Tom Thomson Mystery.* Toronto: McGraw-Hill, 1970.

Mallen, Cheryl. *Canoe Ontario.* Toronto: Canoe Ontario, 1983.

Mason, Bill. *Path of the Paddle.* Toronto: Van Nostrand Reinhold, 1980.

Newcomb, Lawrence. *Newcomb's Wildflower Guide.* Boston: Little, Brown & Co., 1977.

Nickels, Nick. *Canoe Canada.* Toronto: Van Nostrand Reinhold, 1976.

Norman, Dean, ed. *The All-Purpose Guide to Paddling.* Matteson, Ill.: Great Lakes Living Press, 1976.

Peterson, Roger Tory. *A Field Guide to the Birds East of the Rockies.* Boston: Houghton Mifflin Co., 1980.

Pimlott, Douglas H., Shannon, J.A., and Kolenosky, G.B. *The Ecology of the Timber Wolf in Algonquin Provincial Park*. Toronto: Ontario Dept. of Lands and Forests, 1977.

Redi, Chris, ed. *AYH Outdoor Food Book*. Pittsburgh: Pittsburgh Council American Youth Hostels, 1977.

Robins, John D. *The Incomplete Angler*. Toronto: Collins, 1943.

Ross, Catherine, Hutton, Deborah, and Dunbar, Pamela. *When the Wilderness Beckons. A Canoe Tripping Handbook*. Cobalt, Ont.: Highway Bookshop, 1981.

Ruck, Wolf. *Canoeing and Kayaking*. Toronto: McGraw-Hill Ryerson, 1974.

Rutstrum, Calvin. *New Way of the Wilderness*. New York: MacMillan Publishing Co., 1973.

————. *North American Canoe Country*. New York: Collier-MacMillan, 1965.

Rutter, Russell J., and Pimlott, Douglas H. *The World of the Wolf*. Philadelphia and New York: J.B. Lippincott Co., 1969.

Saunders, Audrey. *Algonquin Story*. Toronto: Ontario Dept. of Lands and Forests, 1969.

Scott, Ian, and Kerr, Mavis. *Canoeing in Ontario*. Toronto: Greey de Pencier, 1977.

Stringer, Omer. *The Canoeist's Manual*. Toronto: Consolidated Amethyst Communications, 1975.

INDEX